The main object the compiler had in publishing this list was to make more generally known the right of the 94th Regiment to its title, badge, and honours, and he is not aware that that right has ever before been publicly represented.

The colours of the regiment are unadorned by any of the emblems of its services, but surely, it only requires a proper representation of the facts of the case, to have them restored. They cannot be denied on the ground that the regiment has been disbanded, or how was it that the 18th Hussars, when re-formed in February 1858, had the words "Peninsula" and "Waterloo" restored to them, after the regiment had been out of existence for 37 years, whilst the 94th was in that position only 5 years? In August 1861 the 42nd Regiment was permitted to assume its old national title—"The Black Watch"—even after a lapse of one hundred and twenty years; and the 70th Regiment has, so late as December 1867, obtained the word "Guadaloupe," fifty-seven years after its services there. If, then, the present little work in authenticating these facts should at all conduce to regain for the regiment its long-deferred honours, the compiler will feel highly compensated for his time and trouble. To forward this object, a friend* of the compiler wrote the record of the regiment, which was published in the UNITED SERVICE MAGAZINE for October, November, and December 1868, and which has been favoured with commendation from several old officers of the corps.

To the following officers and gentlemen the compiler tenders his best thanks for the information they have supplied him with, and particularly to Messrs. Thornton and Rutherford, the only officers now living, who served with the "Scotch Brigade" in the Peninsula, and have both reached the age of 80.

Lieut.-General CHARLES GASCOYNE, Colonel of the 89th Regiment.
Lieut.-Colonel WILLIAM HAWLEY FISK, Plymouth Volunteer Rifles.
Major GEORGE DOWDEN DICKSON CLEVELAND, 98th Regiment.
Major EDWARD SMYTH MERCER, 85th Regiment.
Major ALEXANDER MACLEAN, Staff Officer of Pensioners.
Major FREDERICK NASSAU DORE, Staff Officer of Pensioners.
Major ROBERT ALDWORTH, North Cork Rifles.
Captain HENRY HAMILTON PRATT, Staff Officer of Pensioners.
Captain JOHN ORR, late of Edinburgh Militia, Lieut. full pay 8th Vet. Batt.
JOHN THORNTON, Esq., "Nivelle Cottage," Liberton, Edinburgh, half pay 42nd Regiment.
JAMES RUTHERFORD, Esq., Dumfries, half pay 23rd Fusiliers.
PHINEAS CHARLES COCKBURN, Esq., Shanganah Castle, Bray, half pay 70th Regiment.
MATTHEW SHEFFIELD CASSAN, Esq., Sheffield House, Queen's County.
ARTHUR E. GUINNESS, Esq., Dublin.

HEADINGLEY, near LEEDS, MAY 4th, 1869,
  The 70th Anniversary of the Capture of Seringapatam.

---

* Mr. W. Wheater, who is also the author of the Record of the 51st Regiment, now in course of publication in the United Service Magazine, and which will be followed by those of other regiments.

LIST OF OFFICERS OF THE SCOTCH BRIGADE,

AS IT FIRST APPEARED IN THE

ARMY LIST OF 1795.

Colonel-in-Chief, FRANCIS DUNDAS.

1ST BATTALION.	2ND BATTALION.	3RD BATTALION.
Lt. Col. Com.	*Lt. Col. Com.*	*Lt. Col. Com.*
George Cuninghame 5 July 1793	Frederick Halket 5 July 1793	Ilay Ferrier 5 July 1793
Major.	*Major.*	*Major.*
Alexander Hume 5 July 1793	John Stedman 5 July 1793	George Lind 5 July 1793
Captains.	*Captains.*	*Captains.*
Alexander Scott 6 July 1793 Tho. Vinc. Reynolds 8 do. Patrick Ewing 9 do. Henry Johnstone 30 May 1794 William Simson 10 June	David Douglas 5 July 1793 John Cameron 6 do. William Gillespie 7 do. Innes Munro 8 do. John Ramsay 9 do.	Colin Dun. Graham 5 July 1793 James Durham 6 do. Alexander Cameron 8 do. Duncan Drummond 9 do. Robert Collier 12 May 1794
Capt. Lieut. and Capt.	*Captain Lieutenant.*	*Captain Lieutenant.*
James Urquhart 10 July 1793	Rowland Duer 16 Apr. 1794	James Douglas 10 July 1793
Lieutenants.	*Lieutenants.*	*Lieutenants.*
James Sinclair 5 July 1793 John Gilfillan 6 do. Andrew Douglas 7 do. Alexander Robertson 9 do. Queensberry Douglas 10 do. *Hon.* David Ramsay 27 do. John Innes 28 do.	Donald Robertson 5 July 1793 James Macbeath 6 do. Robert Kennedy 7 do. John Turnbull 8 do. William Macbeath 9 do. James Stuart 10 do. John Cambell 25 May 1794	James Gibson 5 July 1793 Francis Simpson do. James Innes 6 do. John Cuninghame 9 do. George Molle 12 May 1794 James Campbell 3 Aug. Donald M'Donell 12 Sep.
Ensigns.	*Ensigns.*	*Ensigns.*
Alexander Campbell 27 July 1794 Thomas Mason 28 do. Colin Campbell 29 do. Hamilton Ross 30 do.	John M'Dougal 5 July 1793 John Robertson 17 Apr. 1794 Hugh Halkett 18 do. Colin Campbell 25 May James Robertson 26 do.	James Campbell 6 July 1793 James Bruce 7 do. Archibald M'Lean 16 Apr. 1794 Charles Beaumont 3 Aug. William Ferrier 4 do. Alexander M'Donald 25 Sep.
Chaplain.	*Chaplain.*	*Chaplain.*
Charles Ochiltree 5 July 1793	David Ritchie 5 July 1793	William Osborn 26 July 1794
Adjutant.	*Adjutant.*	*Adjutant.*
Andrew Douglas 19 Feb. 1794	Robert Kennedy 5 July 1793	James Campbell 14 May 1794
Quarter-Master.	*Quarter-Master.*	*Quarter-Master.*
Thomas Mason 5 July 1793	James Johnston 4 Jan. 1794	John Evers 16 Apr. 1793
Surgeon.	*Surgeon.*	*Surgeon.*
Charles Anderson 5 July 1793	James Anderson 5 July 1793	John D. Robertson 21 May 1794

COLONELS.

FRANCIS DUNDAS, *Ensign*, 4th April, 1775, 1st Foot Guards; *Lieut.* and *Captain*, 23rd Jan., 1778, 1st Foot Guards; *Captain* and *Lieut. Colonel*, 11th April, 1783, 1st Foot Guards; exchd. to 45th Regt., 6th June, 1783; exchd. to 1st Foot, 31st March, 1787; (aptd. Governor of Carrickfergus, 1787) *Colonel*, 12th Oct., 1793; *Colonel in Chief* of the 2th Batt. of the Scotch Brigade, 9th Oct., 1794; *Major General*, 26th Feb., 1795; *Lieut. General*, 29th April, 1802; (made 94th Regt., 1803); aptd. Colonel of the 71st Regt., 7th Jan., 1809; *General*, 1st Jan., 1812; aptd. Governor of Dumbarton Castle, 30th Jan., 1817, died in Scotland, 16th January, 1824.
    Joined the army in North America in May 1777, and was present at the battles of Brandywine and Germantown, and at the siege of ten forts before the close of the campaign on the river Delaware; in 1778, was present in the action at Monmouth; in 1780, commanded his company at the battles of Guildford, and at York Town; present at the siege of Martinique in 1794.

    JAMES, Lord FORBES, *Ensign*, 13th June, 1781, Coldstream Guards; *Lieut.* and *Captain*, 21st April, 1786, Coldstream Guards; *Colonel*, 3rd May, 1796; *Major General*, 29th April, 1802; aptd. Colonel of the 3rd Garr. Batt., 19th July, 1807; *Lieut. General*, 25th April, 1808; aptd. Colonel of the 94th, 7th Jan., 1809; aptd. Colonel of the 54th Regt., 18th Sept., 1809; aptd Colonel of the 21st Fusiliers, 1st June, 1816; *General*, 12th Aug., 1819; died at Bregeny, Lake Constance, 4th May, 1843.
    Served in Flanders, and was present at the following battles and sieges:—viz., Farmars, Valenciennes, Dunkirk, Lincelles, Mouveaux, Tournay, Vaux, Cateau, Nimeguen, Fort St. André; expedition to the Helder, 1799, and was present in every action but one which took place in that campaign.

    WM ROWLAND, Lord HILL, G.C.B., G.C.H., K.C., *Ensign*, 31st July, 1790, 38th Regt; *Lieut.*, 24th Jan., 1791, Indept. Comp.; exchd. to 53rd Regt, 16th March, 1791; *Captain*, 23rd March, 1793, Indept. Comp.; aptd. to 86th Regt., 30th Oct., 1793; *Major*, 10th Feb., 1794, 90th Regt.; *Lieut. Colonel*, 13th May, 1794, 90th Regt.; *Colonel*, 1st Jan., 1800; *Major General*, 30th Oct,, 1805; aptd. Colonel of the 3rd Garr. Batt., 7th Jan., 1809; aptd. Colonel of the 94th, 18th Sept., 1809; *Lieut. General*, 1st Jan., 1812; aptd. Governor of Hull, 13th July, 1814; aptd. Colonel, of the 72nd Regt., 29th April, 1815; aptd. Colonel of the 53rd Regt., 24th Feb., 1817; *General*, 27th May, 1825; aptd. Governor of Plymouth, 18th June, 1830; aptd. Colonel of the Royal Horse Guards, 19th Nov., 1830; died at Hardwick Grange, Shropshire, 10th Dec., 1842. (*Gold Medal for 2, 3, 5, 7, 18, 19, 22, 24, 25.*)

    WM COLVILE, Hon Sir CHARLES, G.C.B., G.C.H., *Ensign*, 6th Dec., 1781, 28th Regt.; *Lieut.*, 30th Sept., 1787, 28th Regt.; *Captain*, 24th Jan., 1791, Indept. Comp.; exchd. to 13th Foot, 18th May, 1791; *Major*, 2nd Sept., 1795, 13th Foot; *Lieut. Colonel*, 26th Aug., 1796, 13th Foot; *Colonel*, 1st Jan., 1805; *Major General*, 25th July, 1810; aptd. Colonel of the 5th Garr. Batt., 10th Oct., 1812; aptd. Colonel of the 94th, 29th April, 1815; *Lieut. General*, 12th Aug., 1819; aptd. Colonel of the 74th Regt., 13th June, 1823; aptd. Colonel of the 14th Foot, 12th Dec., 1834; aptd. Colonel of the 5th Foot, 25th March, 1835; *General*, 10th Jan., 1837; died at Hampstead, 27th March, 1843. (*Gold Medal for Egypt.*) (*Gold Medal for 6, 11, 15, 18, 22.*)
    Served in St. Domingo in 1793-5, and was wounded at the landing; present in most of the affairs that took place; served during the Irish rebellion; expedition to Ferrol; expedition to Egypt 1801, present in the action on landing 8th March, and in those of the 13th and 21st of that month; wounded at Badajoz and Vittoria.

    BRADFORD, Sir THOMAS, G.C.B., G.C.H., *Ensign*, 20th Oct., 1793, Indept. Comp.; *Lieut.*, 9th Dec., 1793, Indept. Comp.; *Captain*, 15th April, 1794, Indept. Comp.; *Major*, 9th Sept., 1795, Nottingham Fencibles; reduced 1795, placed on h. p. of the Regt.; *Bt. Lieut. Colonel*, 1st Jan., 1801; aptd. to 3rd Garr. Batt., 25th Feb., 1805; aptd. to 87th Regt., 30th May, 1805; *Lieut. Colonel*, 18th May, 1809, 34th Regt.; exchd. to 82nd Regt., 21st Dec., 1809; *Colonel*, 25th July, 1810; *Major General*, 4th June, 1813; aptd. Colonel of the 94th Regt., 1st Dec., 1823; *Lieut. General*, 27th May, 1825; aptd. Colonel of the 30th Regt., 16th April, 1829; *General*, 23rd Nov., 1841; aptd. Colonel of the 4th Foot., 7th Feb., 1846; died in Eaton Square, London, 28th Nov., 1853. (*Gold Medal for 5, 16, 18; 20, 24.*)
    Served during the Irish Rebellion; expedition to Hanover, 1805; expedition to South America; present at the siege of Monte Video, and attack on Buenos Ayres; present at the battle of Vimiera, siege of Burgos, assault of Tolosa, passage of the Adour, investment of Bayonne, and repulse of the sortie, at which he was severely wounded.

vi   COLONELS.

JOHN, *Lord* KEANE, G.C.B., G.C.H., *Ensign*, 31st July, 1793, 17th Foot; *Lieut.*, 29th April, 1793, Indept. Co.; *Captain*, 12th Nov., 1794, h. p. of 73rd Regt; exchd. to 44th Regt., 7th Nov., 1799; *Major*, 27th May, 1802, 60th Regt.; *Lieut. Colonel*, 20th Aug., 1803, 13th Foot; *Colonel*, 1st Jan., 1812; aptd. to 60th Regt, 25th June, 1812; *Major General*, 4th June, 1814; aptd. Colonel of the 94th, 18th April, 1829; *Lieut. General*, 22nd July, 1830; aptd. Colonel of the 68th Regt., 13th April, 1831; aptd. Colonel of the 46th Regt., 6th April, 1838; aptd. Colonel of the 43rd Regt., 1st Aug., 1839; died at Burton Lodge, Hampshire, 26th August, 1844. (*Medal for Egypt.*) (*Gold Medal for* 6, 18, 19, 22, 25, 26.) (*Medal for Ghuznee.*)

Served the Egyptian campaign of 1801, as aide-de-camp to the Earl of Cavan. Commanded the 13th regiment at the capture of Martinique in 1809. Joined the Duke of Wellington's army at Madrid, in 1812, and was immediately appointed to command a brigade in the 3rd division, in which corps he served until the end of the war with France, in 1814, and was present at the battles of Vittoria, Pyrenees, Nivelle, near Bayonne, and Orthes; action at Vic Bigorre, battle of Toulouse, and several minor affairs. In Aug. 1814, appointed to command a corps ordered for a particular service; and on arrival at Jamaica, being senior officer, assumed the command of the army destined to co-operate with Vice-Admiral the Hon. Sir Alex. Cochrane, for the attack on New Orleans and the Province of Louisiana. On the morning of the 23rd Dec. effected a landing within nine miles of New Orleans, and that night, with only 1,800 bayonets on shore, repulsed a serious attack of 5,000 of the enemy, assisted by three large armed vessels on their flank. Superseded on the 25th by the arrival of Major-General Sir Edward Packenham, who took the command of the army. Appointed, on the 26th, to the 3rd Brigade, and was present at the affairs of the 28th Dec. and 1st Jany. as also at the assault made on the enemy's fortified lines on the morning of the 8th Jany. 1815, when he was severely wounded in two places. Commanded the army in the field, during the campaign in Affghanistan and Beloochistan, and was present at the assault and capture of Ghuznee. For these services he was raised to the peerage in Dec. 1839.

CAMPBELL, *Sir* JAMES, K.C.B., *Ensign*, 30th Nov., 1791, 1st Foot; *Lieut.*, 20th March, 1794, 1st Foot; *Captain*, 2nd Argyle Fencibles; *Major*, 3rd Jan., 1799, 2nd Argyle Fencibles; exchd. to 94th Regt., 7th April, 1802; *Lieut.-Colonel*, 27th Sept., 1804; *Colonel*, 4th June, 1813; Regt. disbanded 24th Dec., 1818; placed on h. p. of it; *Major General*, 12th Aug., 1819; aptd. Colonel of the 94th, 13th April, 1831; aptd. Colonel of the 74th Regt., 12th Dec., 1834; died in Paris, 6th May, 1835. (*Gold Medal for* 11, 14, 15, 16, 18.) (*Order of the Tower and Sword.*) (*For Services see p.* 10.)

☫ JOHN, *Lord* SEATON, G.C.B., G.C.M.G., G.C.H., *Ensign*, 10th July, 1794, 20th Regt.; *Lieut.*, 4th Sept., 1795, 20th Regt.; *Captain*, 12th Jan., 1800, 20th Regt; *Major*, 21st Jan., 1808, 20th Regt.; *Lieut. Colonel*, 2nd Feb., 1809, 5th Garr. Batt; exchd. to 66th Regt., 2nd Nov., 1809; exchd. to 52nd Regt., 18th July, 1811; *Colonel*, 4th June, 1814; *Major General*, 27th May, 1825; aptd. Colonel of the 94th, 12th Dec., 1834; aptd. Colonel of the 26th Regt., 28th March, 1838; *Lieut. General*, 28th June, 1838; aptd. Colonel of the 2nd Life Guards, 25th March, 1854; *General*, 20th June, 1854; *Field Marshal*, 1st April, 1860; died at Valetta, Torquay, 17th April, 1863. (*Gold Medal for* 5, 12, 14, 22, 24, 25, 26.) (*Silver Medal for* 1, 4, 9, 19.)

Served with the army in North Holland in the campaign of 1799; in Egypt in 1801; and with the British and Russian troops employed on the Neapolitan frontier in 1805. Served in Sicily and Calabria in the campaign of 1806, and was at the battle of Maida. Was Military Secretary to General Fox, Commander of the Forces in Sicily and the Mediterranean in 1806 and 1807, and to Sir John Moore—in Sicily, Sweden, and Portugal, and in Spain in the campaign of 1808-9, and at the battle of Corunna. Joined the army of Lord Wellington in 1809 in Spain at Jaracejo and was sent to La Mancha to report on the operations of the Spanish armies,—was at the battle of Ocana. Commanded a brigade in Sir Rowland Hill's Division in the campaigns of 1810 and 1811, and was detached in command of the Brigade to Castel Branco to observe the movements of General Reynier's Corps d'Armée on the frontier of Portugal. Commanded a Brigade at the battle of Busaco and on the retreat to the Lines of Torres Vedras, and occupied with this Brigade—outside the Lines—the town of Alhandra and the advanced posts near Villa Franca during the time the army was in this position, and afterwards when Massena retired from the front of the Lines. Crossed the Tagus and had charge of the posts on that river opposite the French Corps at the confluence of the Zezere till the evacuation of Portugal by Massena. Commanded the advanced guard of Infantry and Cavalry at the combat of Campo Mayor in Portugal, and was detached in command of a Brigade and force of Artillery and Cavalry with orders to drive back the French outposts during the siege of Badajoz in 1811. Commanded a Brigade at the battle of Albuhera. In 1812 on the investment of Ciudad Rodrigo, commanded the force of the Light Division which stormed the Redoubt of San Francisco on the greater Teson, and the 52nd Light Infantry on the assault of the fortress and town. In 1813 commanded the 2nd Brigade of the Light Division at the attack of the French position and intrenched camp on the heights of Vera, at the battles of the Nivelle and the Nive, and during the operations of the campaign in the Basque Pyrenees. Led the attack of the 52nd Light Infantry on Marshal Soult's position at the battle of Orthes in 1814. Commanded the 2nd Brigade of the Light Division at the combats of Vic Bigorre and Tarbes, and the 52nd at the battle of Toulouse. Was appointed Prince Regent's Aide de Camp in 1814 and Military Secretary to the Prince of Orange, Commander in Chief of the British Forces in the Netherlands. In 1815, commanded the 52nd Light Infantry at the battle of Waterloo, and a Brigade on the March to Paris. Has held the following appointments.—Lieut. Governor of Guernsey; Lieut. Governor of Upper Canada, Commander of the Forces in Canada; Governor General of British North America; Lord High Commissioner to the Ionian Islands; and Commander of the Forces in Ireland. Has received the Grand Cross of the Bath, and of Hanover, and of St. Michael and St. George; the Order of Maria Theresa of Austria, of the Tower and Sword of Portugal, and of St. George of Russia. Was severely wounded at Ciudad Rodrigo.

MCMAHON, *Sir* THOMAS *Bt.*, K.C.B., *Ensign*, 2nd Feb., 1797, 22nd Regt.; *Lieut.*, 24th Oct., 1799, 40th Regt.; aptd. to 32nd Regt., 9th July, 1802; *Captain*, 8th Oct., 1803, 16th Batt. of Reserve; aptd. to 82nd Regt., 14th Aug., 1804; *Major* 6th Nov., 1806, 15th Foot.; placed on h. p. of it; ex. to 2nd West India, April, 1809; *Lt. Col.*, 4th May. 1809, Spanish and

COLONELS. vii

Portuguese Staff; aptd. to 17th Foot, 20th June, 1811 ; *Colonel*, 4th June, 1814 ; placed on h. p. of the Regt.; 25th Dec., 1822 ; *Major General*, 27th May, 1825 ; aptd. Colonel of the 94th, 28th March, 1838 ; *Lieut. General*, 28th June, 1838 ; aptd. Colonel of the 10th Foot, 28th Sept., 1847 ; *General*, 20th June, 1854 ; died at 10, Great Cumberland-street, Hyde Park, 10th April, 1860.
    Served with the expedition under Sir Ralph Abercromby in 1800, destined for operations on the coast of Spain at Cadiz, Ferrol, &c., and subsequently at the occupation of Malta; in the Peninsula in 1809, 10, 11, and part of 1812.

    𝔐 WARRE, Sir WILLIAM, C.B., *Ensign*, 5th Nov., 1803, 52nd Regt.; *Lieut.*, 2nd June, 1804, 52nd Regt.; *Captain*, 25th April, 1806, 98th Regt.; exchd. to 23rd L. D., 7th August, 1806 ; placed on h. p. of the Regt., 25th Nov., 1807 ; *Bt. Major*, 30th May, 1811 ; *Bt. Lieut. Colonel*, 13th May, 1813 ; aptd. Deputy Quarter Master General at the Cape, same day ; *Major* and Permanent Assistant Quarter Master General, 3rd July, 1823 ; *Colonel*, 22nd July, 1830 ; *Lieut. Colonel*, 14th Dec., 1832 ; placed on h. p. Unatt., 1st April, 1837 ; *Major General*, 23rd Nov., 1841; aptd. Colonel of the 94th Regt., 28th Sept., 1847 ; *Lieut. General*, 11th Nov., 1851 ; died in York, 26th July, 1853. (*Silver Medal for 2, 3, 5, 14, 15, 16.*)
    Served the campaign of 1808-9, on the Staff of Sir Ronald Fergusson and Lord Beresford; in March, 1809, accompanied Lord Beresford to Lisbon, as his first Aide-de-camp, and assisted in training the Portuguese troops; served in the field, under his Lordship's orders until May, 1813, and was present at the passage of the Douro, when he was sent to command the peasantry, and to destroy the bridges in rear of the French army under Marshal Soult, the accomplishment of which enabled the advance guard of the British to overtake and defeat the rear of the French at Salamonde, who lost there their remaining guns and baggage ; present during the retreat from the Coa to the lines of Torres Vedras.

    𝔐 STAVELEY, WILLIAM, C.B., *Ensign*, 14th July, 1804, Royal Staff Corps ; *Lieut.*, 21st April, 1808, Royal Staff Corps; *Captain*, 6th May, 1813, Royal African Corps ; *Bt. Major*, 15th Dec., 1814 ; exchd. back to Staff Corps, 12th Jan., 1815 ; *Bt. Lieut. Colonel*, 18th June, 1815 ; exchd. to h. p. Unatt., 29th Sept., 1825 ; aptd. same day Deputy Quarter Master General at the Mauritius ; *Colonel*, 10th Jan., 1837 ; *Major General*, 9th Nov., 1846 ; aptd. Colonel of the 94th Regt., 1st Aug., 1853 ; died at Ootacamund, 4th April, 1854. (*Silver Medal for 7, 11, 14, 15, 18, 22, 24, 26.*)
    Joined the army at Oporto, May, 1809; present at Pombal, Redinha, Foz d'Arouce, Sierra de Moita, Osma, and Morillas; passage of the Bidassoa, storming the heights of Vera, action at Saare; passage of the Adour, storming St. Etienne, and investment of Bayonne; actions at Vic Bigorre and Tarbes; campaign of 1815, including Waterloo, and the capture of Paris.

    THOMAS, HENRY, C.B., *Ensign*, 1st April, 1798, 41st Regt.; *Lieut.*, 29th Dec., 1798, 41st Regt.; placed on h. p. of it 1802 ; aptd. to 44th Regt., 9th July, 1803 ; *Captain*, 10th Sept., 1805, 27th Regt.; *Bt. Major*, 26th Aug., 1813 ; *Bt. Lieut. Colonel*, 21st Jan., 1819 ; *Major*, 16th Dec., 1824, 21st Fusiliers ; *Lieut. Colonel*, 26th Oct., 1825, Unatt. ; exchd. to 20th Regt., 12th Jan., 1826 ; *Colonel*, 10th Jan., 1837 ; exchd. to h. p. Unatt.; 7th Sept., 1841 ; *Major General*, 9th Nov., 1846 ; aptd. Colonel of the 94th, 31st May, 1854 ; *Lieut. General*, 20th June, 1854 ; aptd Colonel of the 20th Regt., 25th July, 1854 ; died at Warrington Lodge, Streatham-common, 21st Sept., 1858. (*Gold Medal for 22, 25, 26.*) (*Silver Medal for 18, 19, 24.*)
    Accompanied Sir James Craig's expedition to Malta and Naples in 1805, and served in Sir James Kempt's Light Battalion. Proceeded thence with the army which took possession of Sicily ; served there four years, and was present at the capture of the Islands of Ischia and Procida. He joined the 3rd Battalion of his Regiment (the 27th) at Escallio in the north of Portugal in April previous to the campaign of 1813, and having command of the Light Company, he was actively employed previous to and at the battle of Vittoria, investment of Pampeluna, battles of the Pyrenees at the Pass of Roncesvalles, heights of Linzoain, heights above Pampeluna, storming of the French position on the 30th July, and pursuit of the enemy until the 6th Aug. 1813; passage of the Bidassoa, heights above Vera. In command of the Light Companies of the right Brigade 4th Division, he commenced the battle of the Nivelle by an attack upon the French advanced redoubt ; in storming their main position his horse was killed under him ; and in following them up drove them out of the village of St Pée. He was also employed in the affairs at Garrett's House and near Bayonne on the 10th and 13th Dec., and when the army was put in motion to repel the enemy's encroachment upon our winter position; also actively employed upon the heights of Bidache. Commanded the above-mentioned Light Companies at the battle of Orthes, battle of Toulouse—the previous day to which he took possession of the bridge over the river Ers, and the village of Croix d'Orade, which had been captured by a charge of the 18th Hussars. Next morning he moved off his post and covered the advance of the divisions upon Mont Blanc, and subsequently covered the flank movement of the columns to turn the right of the enemy, and also the advance of the division till it crowned the heights (horse killed under him) ; he then drove in the enemy's skirmishers, and took up a line to cover the columns till night. After the termination of the Peninsular war he embarked at Bordeaux with the 1st Battalion 27th Regt. for Canada; was present in all the operations on Lake Champlain, and covered the retreat from Plattsburg to Montreal. He was afterwards present at the capture of Paris, and served in France with the Army of Occupation.

    BUTLER, *Hon.* HENRY EDWARD, *Ensign*, 15th Feb., 1800, 85th Regt.; *Lieut.*, 21st June, 1800, 27th Regt.; *Captain*, 22nd May, 1804, 98th Regt.; *Major*, 30th May, 1811, 98th Regt.; exchd. to 4th Garr. Batt., 19th March, 1812; aptd. to the 67th Regt., 21st Dec., 1815 ; *Lieut. Colonel*, 4th July, 1816, 2nd Garr. Batt.; placed on h. p. of it, 25th Dec., 1816 ; *Colonel*, 10th Jan., 1837 ; *Major General*, 9th Nov., 1846 ; *Lieut. General*, 20th June, 1854 ; aptd. Colonel of the 94th Regt., 25th July, 1854 ; aptd. Colonel of the 55th Regt., 29th Jan., 1855; died in Paris, 7th Dec., 1856. (*Turkish Gold Medal for Egypt*.) (*Silver Medal for 9, 27.*)

COLONELS.

HIGGINSON, GEORGE POWELL, *Ensign*, 6th Nov., 1805, 1st Foot Guards; *Lieut. & Captain,* 3th April, 1811, 1st Foot Guards; *Capt. & Lt. Colonel,* 26th Oct., 1820, Grenadier Guards; exchd. to h. p. Unatt., 11th April, 1834; *Colonel,* 10th Jan., 1837; *Major General,* 9th Nov., 1846; *Lieut. General,* 20th June, 1854; aptd. Colonel of the 94th, 29th Jan., 1855; *General,* 9th Nov., 1862; died at Cannes, 19th April, 1866. (*Silver Medal for 5, 20, 22, 24.*)

Served in Sicily, 1807; Walcheren expedition 1809; present at the passage of the Adour, and investment of Bayonne.

WALKER, EDWARD WALTER FORESTIER, C.B., *Ensign & Lieut.*, 8th March, 1827, 3rd Foot Guards; *Lieut. & Capt.,* 18th Oct., 1831, Scots Fusilier Guards; *Captain & Lieut. Colonel,* 6th Dec., 1844, Scots Fusilier Guards; *Colonel,* 20th June, 1854; *Major,* same day; *Lieut. Colonel,* 14th June, 1858; *Major General,* 26th Dec., 1859; aptd. Colonel of the 94th, 20th April, 1866; *Lieut. General,* 19th April, 1868. (*Medal for the Crimea.*) (*Order of the Legion of Honour.*) (*Sardinian Medal.*) (*3rd Class of the Medjidie.*)

Landed in the Crimea, 22nd September, 1854, and commanded the Scotch Fusilier Guards in the subsequent campaign, including the battles of Balaklava and Inkerman (received three wounds, one severe, and had his horse shot under him) siege of Sebastopol (wounded) and repulse of the sortie, 25th October.

THE NINETY-FOURTH REGIMENT IS ENTITLED TO BEAR ON ITS COLOURS

"The Elephant,"

WITH THE WORDS

"SERINGAPATAM,"
"CIUDAD RODRIGO,"   "BADAJOZ,"
"SALAMANCA,"   "VITTORIA,"
"NIVELLE,"   "ORTHES,"
"TOULOUSE,"   "PENINSULA,"

(*London Gazette* No. 17338, *for* 7*th March*, 1818, *page* 426.
,,   No. 17375, *for* 4*th July*,   1818,   ,,   1193.)

KEY TO THE MEDALS.

A *List of Battles and Actions for which Silver Medals were granted under the General Order of the 1st June, 1847, viz.:*—

1 Maida ... . 4th July, 1806.
2 Roleia ... ... 17th August, 1808.
3 Vimiera ... ... 21st August, 1808.
4 Sahagun, Benevente, &c., (*Actions of Cavalry*)   December 1808, and January 1809.
5 Corunna ... ... 16th January, 1809.
6 Martinique (*Attack and Capture*) ... ... February, 1809.
7 Talavera de la Reyna ... ... 27th and 28th July, 1809.
8 Guadaloupe (*Attack and Capture*) .. ... January and February, 1810.
9 Busaco ... ... 27th September, 1810.
10 Barrosa ... ... 5th March, 1811.
11 Fuentes d'Onor ... ... 5th May, 1811.
12 Albuhera ... ... 16th May, 1811.
13 Java (*Attack and Capture*)... ... ... August and September, 1811.
14 Ciudad Rodrigo (*Assault and Capture*) ... January and February, 1812.
15 Badajoz (*Assault and Capture*) ... ... 11th March and 6th April, 1812.
16 Salamanca ... ... 22nd July, 1812.
17 Fort Detroit (*Capture of*), America .. ... August, 1812.
18 Vittoria... ... ... 21st June, 1813
19 Pyrenees ... ... 28th July to 2nd Aug., 1813.
20 St. Sebastian (*Assault and Capture*) ... Aug. and Sept., 1813.
21 Chateauguay, America ... ... 26th October, 1813.
22 Nivelle ... ... 10th November, 1813.
23 Chrystler's Farm, America ... ... 11th November, 1813.
24 Nive ... ... 9th to 13th December, 1813.
25 Orthes ... ... 27th February, 1814.
26 Toulouse ... ... 10th April, 1814.
27 Egypt ... ... 1801.

☛ denotes the medal for Waterloo ; the * before a name, temporary rank in the army. Where no Regt. is stated the 94th is always understood.

NAME.	ENSIGN, &c.	LIEUTENANT.
Addison Thomas Fenn Served in the American war on the staff of Sir John Sherbrooke.	4th May 1800, 1st Dragoon Guards	17th Dec. 1802, 1st Dragoon Guards
Agar John	23rd Aug., 1827, 16th Lancers	5th Jan., 1829, 16th Lancers
Aldworth Robert	15th January, 1829	5th April, 1833
Alexander John	2nd March, 1815, 27th Regt., placed on h. p. of it, 25th July, 1817 ; aptd. to 1st Vt. Batt., 25th Oct., 1822 ; aptd. to 94th, 1st Dec., 1823	8th April, 1825
Allan James, C.B. (*Medal for Seringapatam.*) (*Gold Medal for Toulouse.*) Present at the capture of the Cape of Good Hope in 1795 and 1806; Mysore campaign of 1799; present at the battle of Mallavelly, and siege of Tranquebar, and the whole of the Polygar wars of 1808; served in the war; present at the defence of Cadiz, Vic Bigorre, and Tarbes.	31st Dec., 1794, Independent Company	18th March, 1795 battle of Blauberg; served in the and storm of Seringapatam, reduction Peninsula from 1810 to the end of
Anderson Charles	19th Oct., 1794, 81st Regt.	29th October, 1794
Anstruther Philip Robert	31st December, 1858	25th May, 1860
Armit John	21st Jan., 1813, 27th Regt.	10th March, 1814, 27th Regt., placed on h. p. of it 25th March, 1817 ; exchd. to 40th Regt., 28th June, 1821, placed on h. p. of it, 25th Aug., 1821 ; aptd. to 94th, 1st December, 1823 ; exchd. to h. p. of 47th Regt., 1st April, 1824
Armstrong Robert	24th August, 1806	... ...
Ashton Thomas Henry	27th September, 1839	31st December, 1841
Atkinson Thomas George Brutton (*Medal for Sebastopol*) (*Turkish Medal.*)	6th June, 1854, 46th Regt.	9th Feb., 1855, 46th Regt.
Aytoun John Marriot	12th January, 1855	31st July, 1857
𝕮𝕮𝕮 Bacon Anthony (*Silver Medal for 22, 24.*) Knight Commander of the Tower and Sword. Wounded, and had his horse killed under him at Waterloo. For full particulars of his services see United Ser. Magazine for Aug. 1864, p. 596.	13th August, 1812, 16th Light Dragoons	11th March, 1813, 16th Light Dragoons ; aptd. to 10th Hussars, 9th February, 1815; placed on h. p. of the Regt., 25th March, 1816 ; aptd. to 13th Light Dragoons, 8th November, 1818
Baird William	31st October, 1798	22nd September, 1800

94TH REGT.

CAPTAIN.	HIGHER RANKS, AND REMARKS.
24th Dec., 1803, 1st Dragoon Guards; exchd. to 94th Regt., 24th Oct., 1811; exchd. to 100th Regt., (altered to 99th, 1816), 5th March, 1812; disbanded, placed on h. p. of it, 25th Nov., 1818	Aptd. Secretary at Annapolis Royal, 1812; Bt. Major, 4th June, 1814; Bt. Lieut. Colonel, 13th October, 1814; Colonel, 10th Jan., 1837; Major General, 9th Nov., 1846; died at Sudbury, Suffolk, 11th Nov., 1852.
11th April, 1834, Unatt.; exchd. to 94th, 2nd October, 1835	Retired 22nd July, 1836.
8th June, 1838	Retired 10th May, 1844; aptd. Captain of the North Cork Militia, 19th January, 1846; Major, 30th June, 1855
... ...	Died at Gibraltar, 11th Sept., 1828.
10th Sept., 1799	Major, 20th July, 1809; Bt. Lieut. Colonel, 4th June, 1814; disbanded, placed on h. p. of the Regt., 25th Dec., 1818; aptd. to f. p. of it, 1st Dec., 1823; Lieut. Colonel, 29th June, 1826, Unatt.; aptd. to 57th Regt., 20th March, 1828; Colonel, 10th Jan., 1837; Major General, 9th Nov., 1846; aptd. Colonel of the 50th Regt., 11th Oct., 1852; died at Cheltenham, 17th Nov., 1853.
26th January, 1804	Killed at Ciudad Rodrigo, 19th Jan., 1812
3rd January, 1865	
... ...	Retired March, 1827; died at Dieppe, 1st June, 1836
... ...	Retired October, 1808
3rd March, 1848, 18th Regt.; exchd. to 44th Regt., 15th February, 1850; aptd. to 57th Regt., 19th April, 1850	Retired 7th March, 1851
1st April, 1857, Unatt.; aptd. to Military Train, 4th Nov., 1859; exchd. to 17th Foot, 22nd June, 1860; exchd. to 94th, 29th March, 1861	Retired 24th November, 1863.
... ...	Killed in action in the Punjaub, 4th May, 1860
11th Oct., 1821; h. p. of 18th Hussars; aptd. to 94th, 1st Dec. 1823	Major, 31st December, 1825, Unatt.; exchd. to 17th Lancers, 8th April, 1826; retired 31st December, 1827; died at Crondall, near Fareham, Hants, 2nd July, 1864
24th April, 1809; exchd. to 11th Foot, 20th June, 1811; aptd. 13th Vt. Batt., 25th Jan., 1813; reduced 1815, placed on retired f. p. of it	Died in Herefordshire, 1st July, 1826

94TH REGT.

NAME.	ENSIGN, &c.	LIEUTENANT.
Balvaird William, C.B. (*Gold Medal for* 22, 24.) (*Silver Medal for* 9, 11, 14, 15, 16, 19.) Severely wounded at Badajoz.	24th March, 1803	17th April, 1804, 78th Regt.
Barwell Osborn (*Silver Medal for* 18, 26.) *Re-entered the Army*	... ... 11th Sept., 1811, 1st Dragoons	9th April, 1807 2nd April, 1812, 1st Dragoons; placed on h. p. of the Regt., 1814; exchd. to 11th Light Dragoons, 22nd Sept., 1820
Basden James Lewis, C.B. (*Medal for Services in the East Indies.*) (*Medal for Ava.*) Mahratta war of 1803, 4, and 5, Chawdore, Jaulnah, and Gawillewhere he was severely wounded in gara; Burmese war of 1824—25.	12th Jan., 1800 including the taking of Berhampore, ghurr; American war in 1813—14, the thigh, Fort Erie, Black Rock,	17th March, 1801 Asseerghur, Argaum, Lasslgaum, and was engaged at Longwoods, Buffalo, and was wounded at Niagara;
Basset Wm. West James (*Medal for the Kaffir war*)	25th April, 1848, 74th Regt.	3rd Aug., 1849, 74th Regt.
Bathurst Henry	17th Nov., 1825	5th April, 1827, 9th Foot
Bayley James Twisleton	16th Aug., 1825, 54th Regt.	29th July, 1828, 54th Regt.; exchd. to 94th, 15th Jan., 1841
Beatley Arthur	15th Sept. 1804	... ...
Beckwith, William	28th Feb., 1800	... ...
Beebee Robert Morris	25th May, 1826, 6th Foot	20th Sept., 1827, 6th Foot
Beet John Goodday	19th April, 1821, 21st Fusiliers	26th Nov., 1825, 21st Fusiliers
Bedford William	18th March, 1813, 5th Garr. Batt.; placed on h. p. of it, 1814; exchd. to 10th Foot, 25th June, 1816; exchd. to 34th Regt., 8th Nov., 1821; placed on h. p. of it; aptd. to 94th, 1st Dec., 1823	25th January, 1825, 2nd Foot; exchd. to h. p. Unatt., 14th June, 1827; exchd. to 48th Regt., 29th October, 1829; placed on h. p. of it, 25th November, 1833
Bell Whiteford John	13th Nov., 1846	23rd March, 1849; aptd. to 74th Regt., 29th July, 1853
Bell William	27th March, 1824, 48th Regt.	23rd March, 1826, 48th Regt.
Bickerton John	29th April, 1813, Waggon Train; placed on h. p. of it, 1814; aptd. to 1st Vt. Batt., 25th October, 1822; aptd. to 94th, 1st Dec., 1823	7th April, 1825; exchd. to h. p. Unatt., 20th Oct., 1825
Birney James	6th Nov., 1817; placed on h. p. of the Regt., 25th Dec., 1818; exchd. to 49th Regt., 8th March, 1821; placed on h. p. of it, 25th Aug. 1821	... ...

94TH REGT.

CAPTAIN.	HIGHER RANKS, AND REMARKS.
16th May, 1805, 100th Regt.; aptd. to 95th Rifles, 15th August, 1805	Bt. Major, 22nd November, 1813 ; Major, 21st July, 1814, 95th Rifles ; Bt. Lieut. Colonel, 21st June, 1817 ; placed on h. p. of the Corps, 25th Dec. 1818 ; aptd. to 99th Regt. 25th March, 1824 : Lieut. Colonel, 1st June, 1826, Unatt.; Colonel, 10th Jan., 1837 ; exchd. to 37th Regt., 27th Aug., 1841 ; retired same day ; died at Edinburgh, 7th Sept., 1853
... ...	Retired 1810
1st Aug., 1826, Unatt.; exchd. to 6th Foot, 14th September, 1826 ; exchd. to h. p. Unatt., 24th January, 1828	
4th Sept., 1806, 89th Regt.	Bt. Major, 30th Dec., 1813 ; Major, 25th Nov., 1821, 89th Regt.; Bt. Lieut. Colonel, 22nd July, 1830 ; Lieut. Colonel, 7th July, 1838, 89th Regt.; retired on f. p. of it, 16th June, 1843'; Colonel, 28th Nov., 1854 ; died at Newton Villa, Westbourne-grove, 22nd May, 1856
29th July. 1853, 74th Regt.; aptd. to 94th, 22nd July, 1854	Bt. Major, 24th October, 1865 ; retired 7th Aug., 1866
11th June, 1830, 9th Foot ; exchd. to 3rd Foot Guards, 12th July, 1831	Captain and Lieut. Colonel, 13th Jan., 1843, 3rd Foot Guards ; retired 24th Nov., 1848
11th April, 1845, Unatt.	Aptd. Adjutant of the Renfrew Militia, 27th Feb., 1846 ; died at Glasgow, 31st January, 1848
... ...	Retired June, 1807
... ...	Retired 30th July, 1800
21st June, 1839, 6th Foot ; exchd. to 40th Regt., 12th Aug., 1839 ; exchd. to 94th, 27th August, 1841	Died at Cannanore, Madras, 7th Oct., 1841
6th Sept., 1831, 21st Fusiliers ; aptd. to 94th, 18th January, 1833 ; exchd. to h. p. of Sub-Inspector of Militia, 2nd Nov., 1838	Died 1839
... ...	Died 14th October, 1864
23rd July, 1858, 9th Foot; exchd. to 93rd Regt., 14th June, 1859	
1st Dec., 1837, 48th Regt.; exhd. to 94th, 13th April, 1838	Died at Madras, 27th March, 1842
... ...	Died 1825
... .	Retired 29th May, 1831

NAME.	ENSIGN, &C.	LIEUTENANT.
Black John	April, 1795	24th Aug., 1795
Blackwell Nathaniel, C.B. (*Gold Medal for 6, 8, 24.*) Present in the Mysore war, and at the storming of Seringapatam ; Capture of the Danish Islands of St. Thomas, and Santa Cruz.	... ...	9th Sept., 1795
Blair David Hunter	4th April, 1845, 26th Regt.	12th Nov., 1847, 26th Regt.; exchd. to 94th, 31st Dec., 1847
Blake Frederic Rudolph, C B.	30th June, 1825, 85th Regt.	14th August, 1827, 85th Regt.; exchd. to 94th, 29th Jan., 1829
Went out in command of his regiment, which he led with distinguished gallantry at the battle of the Alma, and continued to serve before Sebastopol, until compelled to return home in consequence of a severe attack of fever, from the effects of which he never recovered.		
Blake John Joseph	29th July, 1859	25th September, 1860 ; exchd. to 86th Regt., 28th April 1863
Bligh John Thomas	28th September, 1830 ; exchd. to 61st Regt, 18th Jan. 1833	5th Feb., 1836, 61st Regt.
Bogue John, K.H.	May, 1808	29th Sept., 1808
Served in the Peninsula from 1810 to 1814, during which period he was present at numerous engagements ; wounded at Ciudad Rodrigo in 1812, and again severely at Badajoz the same year.		
Boileau Isaac Spencer Baré Phipps	29th April, 1842, 22nd Regt.	29th Dec., 1843, 22nd Regt.; aptd. to 94th, 25th April, 1845
Bogle James, C.B. (*Gold Medal for 15, 22.*)	... ...	10th Feb., 1796
Bowlby Geo. Russell Salvin	20th May, 1864	7th August, 1866
Bowles Francis William	14th Sept., 1832, 39th Regt.; aptd. to 83rd Regt., 21st September, 1832	10th June, 1836, 83rd Regt.; exchd. to 94th, 11th Aug., 1837
Bredin George Noble	6th August, 1841, 26th Regt.	30th September, 1843, 1st West India ; aptd. to 98th Regt., 8th August, 1845 ; exchd. to 94th, 1st December, 1846.
Brinckman Arthur	11th May, 1855	15th January, 1858
Bringhurst John Dorset	27th March, 1806, 1st D. G.	1st January, 1807, 1st D. G.
Slightly wounded at Vittoria, where he served as Aide-de-Camp to Major General Fane.		
Brockman Charles Henry	20th September, 1864, Military Train ; exchd. to 94th, 23rd March, 1866	
Brook Edmund Smith	7th August, 1866	
Brooke Henry Francis (*Medal for Sebastopol.*) (*Turkish Medal*) (*Medal for China.*)	6th June, 1854, 63rd Regt.; aptd. to 48th Regt. 23rd June, 1854	15th May, 1855, 48th Regt.
Landed with the 48th Regt. in the Crimea on the 21st April, 1855, and served at the siege and fall of Sebastopol. Served throughout the campaign of 1860 in China as Aide de Camp to Sir Robert Napier, and was present at the actions of Sinho and Tongkoo, the assault of the Taku forts (severely wounded), and the final advance on, and surrender of Pekin.		
Brown James	15th June, 1815, 57th Regt.; placed on h. p. of it, 25th Feb., 1816 ; exchd. back to f. p. of it, 28th March, 1816	5th October, 1820, 57th Regt. placed on h. p. of it, 25th Oct., 1821 ; exchd. back to f. p. of it, 17th Jan., 1822

CAPTAIN.	HIGHER RANKS, AND REMARKS.
... ...	Died 1800
11th Dec., 1800, 60th Regt.; aptd. to 41st Regt., 25th Dec. 1802	Major, 27th Feb., 1806, 1st West India; Lt. Colonel, 4th April, 1808, 4th West India; aptd. to 62nd Regt., 13th June, 1811; Colonel, 4th June, 1814; placed on h. p. of the Regt., 25th May, 1817; Major-General, 27th May, 1825; died at Cheltenham, 28th August, 1833
5th Jan., 1855, Unatt.; aptd. to Scots Fusilier Guards, 8th Feb., 1856	Retired 8th January, 1864
23rd August, 1831; aptd. to 33rd Regt., 18th Jan., 1833	Major, 14th April, 1843, 33rd Regt.; Lieut. Colonel, 3rd Oct., 1848, 33rd Regt.; Colonel, 28th Nov., 1854; died at Rottingdean, Sussex, 23rd Aug., 1855
2nd Dec., 1842, 61st Regt.	Died at Kussowlie, 21st October, 1847
17th Feb., 1814; placed on h. p. of the Regt., 25th Dec., 1818; exchd. to 27th Regt., 8th January, 1820	Major, 19th September, 1826, Unatt.; died at Coldingham, Berwickshire, 4th January, 1838
... ...	Died at Cannanore, 7th June, 1852
14th May, 1805; placed on h. p. of the Regt., 25th Dec., 1818; reaptd. to f. p. of it, 1st Dec., 1823	Bt. Major, 26th August, 1813; Bt. Lieut. Colonel, 22nd July, 1830; Major, 3rd August, 1830, Unatt.; died in Edinburgh, 31st December, 1835
... ...	Died at Bombay, 17th August, 1841
... ...	Retired 24th January, 1851; drowned in the river Demarara, 2nd May, 1852
... ...	Retired 25th September, 1860
18th July, 1811; exchd. back to 1st D. G., 24th Oct, 1811	Bt. Major 12th April, 1814; killed at Waterloo, 18th June, 1815
24th Sept., 1858, 48th Regt.; exchd. to 94th, 30th January, 1865	Bt. Major, 15th February, 1861
28th Sept., 1830, 57th Regt.	Major, 11th Feb., 1842, 57th Regt.; exchd. to 94th, 6th May, 1843; Lieut. Colonel, 9th Nov., 1846; exchd. to 43rd Regt., 21st April, 1854; Colonel, 20th June, 1854; died at Bellary, 6th November, 1856

NAME.	ENSIGN, &c.	LIEUTENANT.
Browne James	30th July, 1859	28th December, 1860
Browne William	27th Sept., 1798, 13th Light Dragoons	3rd May, 1800, 13th Light Dragoons
Bruce Robert (*Medal for the Kaffir war.*)	9th June, 1838	22nd May, 1840 ; exchd. to 97th Regt., 12th March, 1841
Buchan *Sir* John, K.C.B. (*Gold Medal for Seringapatam.*) (*Gold Medal for* 8, 18, 19, 22, 24.) (*Silver Medal for* 25, 26.) Served in the Mysore war, present at the battle of Malavelley, and assault of Seringapatam ; operations against the Southern Polygars ; also in the Kandian war.	29th July, 1795	21st October, 1795
Buchanan James	20th Aug., 1844	25th Aug., 1847
Budd Claud Currie	24th January, 1865	
Buller Henry George	26th June, 1835	8th June, 1838
Buller Walter Gregory	30th Sept., 1859	22nd February, 1861
Bunbury Robert Henry	31st August, 1815, 88th Regt.; placed on h. p. of the Regt., 25th March, 1816 ; exchd. to 91st Regt., 22nd March, 1821 ; exchd. to h. p. of 37th Regt., 3rd May, 1821 ; aptd. to 2nd Vet. Batt., 13th Feb., 1823 ; aptd. to 95th Regt., 1st December, 1823	7th April, 1825, 95th Regt.: exchd. to h. p. of 70th Regt.; 8th Sept., 1825 ; aptd. to 66th Regt., 13th March, 1827 ; aptd. to 94th Regt., 22nd Oct., 1828 ; exchd. to h. p. Unatt., 25th May, 1832 ; exchd. to 96th Regt., 17th Aug., 1832 ; exchd. to h. p. of 38th Regt., 22nd July, 1836
Burke Thomas	8th August 1822, 20th Regt.	5th October, 1826, 20th Regt.; exchd. to 4th Foot, 18th Jan., 1839 ; aptd. to 94th, 22nd October, 1839
Burns Matthew	2nd February, 1797	11th October, 1800, 84th Regt.
Burslem George James	10th Sept., 1825, 43rd Regt.	31st August, 1826, 44th Regt.
Burton Wm. Kinninmond	31st March, 1804, 15th Foot; aptd. to 22nd L. D., 30th June 1804	1st June, 1806, 22nd L. D.; exchd. to 80th Regt., 2nd Jan., 1807 ; exchd. to 94th 22nd Sept., 1807 ; exchd. to 4th Garr. Batt., 30th Nov., 1809 ; placed on h. p. of it, 1814
Butler Charles	19th August, 1856	14th March, 1859
Butler, Theobald (*Silver Medal for* 2, 3, 16, 19, 22, 24, 25.)	8th Oct., 1806, 32nd Regt.	28th April, 1808, 32nd Regt.: exchd. to h. p. of 14th Foot, 22nd June, 1820 ; aptd. to 94th, 22nd June, 1832
Cafe Haydon Lloyd	27th September, 1844, 1st West India	9th December, 1845, 1st West India

94TH REGT.

CAPTAIN.	HIGHER RANKS, AND REMARKS.
2nd October, 1866	
24th May, 1804, 13th Light Dragoons; exchd. to 28th Regt., 13th June, 1805; exchd. to 94th, 4th July, 1805	Major, 8th Sept., 1808, 5th West India; died July, 1812
21st July, 1848, 97th Regt.; exchd. to 74th Regt., 4th August, 1848	Bt. Major, 28th May, 1853; Major, 5th Sept., 1856, Unatt.; aptd. to a Depôt Batt., 1st Oct., 1856; Lieut. Colonel, 12th May, 1857, Unatt.; aptd. to 2nd Foot, 14th Aug., 1857; retired on h. p. of the Regt., 19th Jan., 1864; Colonel, 17th May, 1867
15th March, 1802, 2nd Ceylon Regt.	Major, 30th June, 1804, 2nd Ceylon Regt.; Lieut. Colonel, 30th March, 1809, 4th West India; aptd. to Portuguese Staff, 25th October, 1814; placed on h. p. of it, 25th Dec. 1816; Colonel, 12th August, 1819; exchd. to 29th Regt., 28th Feb., 1822; exchd. to h. p. Unatt., 10th June, 1826; Major-General, 22nd July, 1830; aptd. Colonel of the 95th Regt., 5th Nov., 1838; Lieut. General, 23rd Nov., 1841; aptd. Colonel of the 32nd Regt., 12th June, 1843; died at 39, Upper Harley-street, London. 2nd June, 1850
18th Sept., 1857	Retired 18th February, 1859
5th June, 1844	Major 1st July, 1854; Lieut. Colonel, 18th Sept., 1857; Colonel, 18th Sept., 1862; died at Delhi, 25th September, 1867
... ...	Died 30th May, 1839
... ...	Died at Cannanore, Madras, 23rd July, 1841
20th May, 1808, 84th Regt.	Retired 20th July, 1820
17th Nov., 1832, 44th Regt.; aptd. to 94th, 26th April, 1834; exchd. to 48th Regt., 13th April, 1838	Retired 8th September, 1838
... ...	Died at Aberdeen, 25th February, 1820
30th June, 1863	
28th Nov., 1834, Unatt.; aptd. to 72nd Regt., 7th Oct., 1851	Bt. Major, 9th Nov. 1846; retired 7th October, 1851
28th December, 1849, 1st West India; exchd. to 94th, 16th May, 1851	Bt. Major, 20th December, 1861; Major, 16th Sept., 1868

B

NAME.	ENSIGN, &c.	LIEUTENANT.
Cairncross Alexander, K.H. Served in the Peninsula from Jan. lines of Torres Vedras, pursuit of battle of Fuentes d'Onor, siege and of Ciudad Rodrigo, siege and storm Fort La China, retreat into Portugal, severely through the right elbow-	25th June, 1803 1810, to October, 1813, including the Massena, actions at Redinha, Pu-blockade of Badajoz, actions at El of Badajoz, battle of Salamanca, and battle of Vittoria; wounded at joint, and lost the use of that arm	15th Sept., 1804 defence of Cadiz, occupation of the denta, Foz d'Arouce, and Sabugal, Boden and Guinaldo, siege and storm capture of Madrid, the Retiro, and Ciudad Rodrigo, and at Vittoria in consequence.
Cameron Donald Meent	26th April, 1828, 16th Foot; aptd. to 3rd Foot, 31st July, 1828	17th March, 1830, 3rd Foot
Campbell Adam	19th April, 1836, 1st West India	19th February, 1838, 1st West India; aptd. to 94th, 22nd October, 1839
Campbell Archibald, C.B. (*Gold Medal for* 6, 18.) Present at the capture of Marti- nique, February, 1809	28th Dec., 1787, 77th Regt.	26th April, 1791, 77th Regt.
Campbell Charles	January, 1798	7th February, 1798
Campbell Charles	2nd August, 1800	3rd Sept., 1803
Campbell Charles (*Silver Medal for* 11, 14, 15, 16, 18, 19, 22, 24, 25, 26.) Present at the defence of Cadiz, at El Boden; capture of Madrid;	27th Sept., 1803, 80th Regt. pursuit of Massena, actions at Re-affair at Vic Bigorre.	17th March, 1804 dinha, Condeixa, and Sabugal; action
Campbell David (*Silver Medal for* 14, 15, 16, 18, 19.)	28th Sept., 1808	17th May, 1810
Campbell Frederick Wounded at Argaum.	27th Feb., 1796, 86th Regt.	23rd February, 1800
Campbell Fred. Buckley	28th July, 1863, 64th Regt., aptd. to 94th, 8th Sept., 1863	3rd April, 1866
Campbell Sir James, K.C.B. (*Gold Medal for* 11, 14, 15, 16, 18.) (*Order of the Tower and Sword.*) Present at the capture of Minorca to March 1806, present at the battle at Chandore was entrusted with banded in 1818. was presented with	30th Nov., 1791, 1st Foot in 1798; Mahratta war under the of Argaum, and at the capture of forcing the enemies outposts and a sword by the Officers. Wounded	20th March, 1794, 1st Foot Duke of Wellington from Jan. 1803 Gaweil Ghur, when he led the attack; batteries. When the Regt. was dis-at Salamanca and at Vittoria.
Campbell James	7th February, 1800	18th March, 1802
Campbell James	September, 1807	25th November, 1808
Campbell John	April, 1794	25th May, 1794
Campbell John	30th June, 1799	... ...
Campbell William Wilson	22nd July, 1842	20th March, 1846
Cannon William (*Silver Medal for* 11, 14, 16, 18, 19, 25, 26.) Present at the defence of Mata-gorda, lines of Torres Vedras, action at El Boden; severely wounded at Ciudad Rodrigo, and slightly at Vittoria.	26th August, 1807	7th June, 1810; placed on h. p. of the Regt., 25th Dec., 1818; aptd. to 97th Regt., 25th March, 1824

94TH REGT.

CAPTAIN.	HIGHER RANKS, AND REMARKS.
7th June, 1810; placed on h. p. of the Regt., 25th Dec., 1818; aptd. to 8th Vet. Batt., 24th Feb., 1820; disbanded, 1821; aptd. to 2nd Vet. Batt., 25th Dec., 1821; aptd. to 96th Regt., 29th January, 1824	Major, 10th June, 1826, 96th Regt.; Lt. Colonel, 19th Sept., 1834, 96th Regt.; retired 22nd July, 1842; died on board the *St. George*, on passage from Sydney, 16th May 1843
12th March 1840, 3rd Foot	Major, 10th Dec., 1847, 3rd Foot; exchd. to 94th, 16th July, 1852; died off St. Helena, on board the *Hampshire*, on passage from India, 30th June, 1854
22nd August, 1849; aptd. to 74th Regt., 26th Jan., 1855; exchd. to h. p. Unatt., 9th January, 1857	Aptd. Staff Officer of Pensioners, 1st July, 1856; Bt. Major, 17th June, 1861; died at Ennis, 26th Dec., 1864
13th August, 1794, 98th Regt., made 91st 1798; exchd. to 94th, 16th June, 1801	Bt. Major, 1st Jan., 1805; Major, 29th Oct., 1807, West India Rangers; Lieut. Colonel, 8th March, 1810, 4th Ceylon Regt.; exchd. to 6th Foot, 17th Sept., 1812; Colonel, 12th Aug., 1819; exchd. to h. p. of 90th Regt., 4th April 1822; Major General, 22nd July, 1830; died at Jersey, 12th May, 1838
22nd August, 1805	Retired 19th April, 1810
25th August, 1809; exchd. to 79th Regt., 18th Jan., 1810; placed on h. p. of it, 12th November, 1812	Died at Glasgow, 6th April, 1836
14th July, 1808	Bt. Major, 12th April, 1814; Major, 16th Feb., 1815; placed on h. p. of the Regt., 25th Dec., 1818; Bt Lt. Colonel, 22nd July, 1830; died at Bath, 17th April, 1852
20th October, 1814; placed on h. p. of the Regt., 25th Dec., 1818; aptd. to 98th Regt., 27th May, 1824	Retired 8th April, 1826; died December, 1848
21st Dec., 1809, 85th Regt.; exchd. back to 94th Regt., 25th Jan., 1813; placed on h. p. of the Regt., 25th Dec., 1818	Died at Campbelltown, Argyleshire, 31st October, 1829
6th Sept., 1794, 42nd Regt.	Major, 3rd Jan., 1799, 2nd Argyle Fenc. Infantry; exchd. to 94th, 7th April, 1802; Lieut. Colonel, 27th Sept., 1804; Colonel, 4th June, 1813; Regt. disbanded, 24th Dec., 1818; placed on h. p. of it; Major General, 12th Aug., 1819; aptd. Colonel of the 94th, 13th April, 1831; aptd. Colonel of the 74th Regt., 12th Dec., 1834; died in Paris, 6th May, 1835
... ...	Killed while acting as Capt. 19th Portuguese Regt., Sept. 1813
28th December, 1796	Major, 2nd July 1803; died in the Mahratta country, Sept. 1804
... ...	Retired 2nd August, 1800
... ...	Retired 10th March, 1848
7th April, 1825, 97th Regt.	Bt. Major, 28th June, 1838; Major, 26th October, 1841, 97th Regt.; retired on f. p. of it, 27th September, 1842; died in Maxwelltown, Dumfriesshire, 15th November, 1851

NAME.	ENSIGN, &c.	LIEUTENANT.
Cardew Henry Clare	8th Jan., 1836, 57th Regt.	14th Dec., 1838, 57th Regt.; aptd. to 94th, 22nd Oct., 1839
Carmichael J. Doddington, C.B. (*Medal for Goojerat.*) (*Medal for Oude.*) Served with the 32nd Regt. at the of Soorjkoond; led the right column and was present at the surrender of and at the battle of Goojerat. Comthe forts of Dehaign and Tyrhool the Nusseerabad Mutineers under able manner in which he commanded manded a moveable column, which, was sent in pursuit of the rebel chief object the column successfully acfor the decision and celerity of his	12th July, 1839, 31st Regt. first and second siege operations of attack at the storm and capture the fortress, as also at the surrender manded the Regt. in the Indian camunder Brigadier Berkeley; again at Brigadier Horsford, and was thanked the Infantry." Served the campaign acting under the orders of and in Beni Maddoo, to drive him and his complished — mentioned in Lord movements."	11th May, 1841, 31st Regt.; exchd. to 32nd Regt., 29th October, 1841 before Mooltan, and was at the action of the city of Mooltan (wounded), of the fort and garrison of Cheniote, paign at the attack and capture of the action of Daodpore and defeat of in that officer's despatch "for the for the reduction of Oude,—comconjunction with Lord Clyde's force, troops across the river Gogra, which Clyde's despatch as "distinguished
Carter Frederick Falconer	27th August, 1825	24th May, 1827
Cassan Matthew Sheffield	6th July, 1820, 93rd Regt.; placed on h. p. of it, 25th Oct., 1821; aptd to 3rd Vet. Batt., 25th Oct., 1822; aptd. to 94th, 7th April, 1825; exchd. to h. p. of 21st Fusiliers, 25th Oct., 1827; aptd. to 16th Foot, 28th March, 1834	... ...
Cavagnari Mont. Charles Adolphe	16th May, 1865, 24th Regt.; aptd. to 94th, 20th Oct., 1865	... ...
Chichester *Hon.* F. Alg. J.	20th July, 1849; Bengal Army; aptd. to 8th Bengal Light Cavalry, 29th Dec., 1849	10th August, 1850, 8th Bengal Light Cavalry
Chute Arthur	4th May, 1855	14th August, 1857
Clegg William	9th October, 1855	5th October, 1858, 11th Foot
Clerke St. John Aug., K.H. (*Silver Medal for* 11, 14, 15.) Served with the 94th at Cadiz, from Santarem; having been present He joined the 77th Regt. (also in the Aldea de Ponte, severely wounded in and his services at Picurina and the superiors.	13th Oct., 1808, 4th Garr. Batt.; ex. to 94th, 24th May, 1810 during the siege, in the Lines of in the actions of Pombal, Redinha, Peninsula) on promotion, and served the right knee at Badajoz. For the storming of Badajoz were voluntary	6th June, 1811, 77th Regt. Torres Vedras, during the retreat Condeixa, Foz d'Arouces, Sabugal, with it in the actions of El Boden and affair at Redinha he was promoted, and were duly recognised by his
Cleveland George Dowden Dickson (*Medal for the Punjaub.*) (*Medal for Nepaul.*) Served in the Punjaub campaign frontier under Sir Sydney Cotton in heights of Sultana on the 4th May; from April to Dec. 1859, and was	10th May, 1844 of 1848-49. Served in the Peshawur April and May 1858, and at the affair raised a levy in 1858, and was actively twice thanked by Government.	2nd Sept., 1845; exchd. to 98th Regt., 19th Feb., 1847 Expeditionary force an the Euzofzie with the Hindostanee fanatics on the employed on the frontier of Nepaul,
Cleveland H. Wahab Baird	28th Dec, 1841, 2nd Foot; aptd. to 94th, 28th Jan., 1842	10th Sept., 1844
Coast Michael Wm. Lade (*Medal for Oude.*) (*Medal for the Crimea.*) (*Turkish Medal*) Served with the Rifle Brigade Lucknow and numerous affairs dur Coates Richard Aylmer	3rd Jan., 1851, 69th Regt.; aptd. to 94th, 24th January, 1851 during the suppression of the Indian ing the Oude campaign. Served in 22nd Oct., 1812, 60th Regt.	21st July, 1854 mutiny, including the capture of the Crimea from Feb. 1855. 27th Jan., 1814, 60th Regt.; placed on h. p. of it, 25th Aug., 1819; exchd. to 94th, 10th Nov., 1825; ex. to h. p. of 47th Regt., 29th Oct., 1829

CAPTAIN.	HIGHER RANKS, AND REMARKS.
... ... 18th April, 1845, 32nd Regt.	Died on board the *Mary Anne*, off the Cape of Good Hope, on passage home from Madras, 24th August, 1847 Major, 20th Feb., 1855, 32nd Regt.; Bt. Lieut. Colonel, 1st Feb., 1856; Lieut. Colonel, 26th Nov., 1857, 32nd Regt.; exchd. to h. p. of 19th Regt., 25th Sept., 1860; aptd. to 94th, 18th Feb., 1862; Colonel, 2nd March 1863 aptd. Deputy Quartermaster General, at Suez, 15th Sept., 1868; placed on h. p. of the Regt., same day
... .	Retired 3rd Dec., 1830; died in Dublin, 13th October, 1849 Retired 11th April, 1834
... ...	Retired 14th October, 1868
16th Sept., 1858, 5th Bengal Light Cavalry, aptd. to 94th, 17th Nov., 1863; exchd. to 7th Hussars, 19th April, 1864	Retired 22nd August, 1865
... ... 11th March, 1819, 77th Regt.	Retired 25th May, 1860 Died at Fort Napier, Natal, 4th February, 1865 Major, 26th May, 1825, 77th Regt.; Lieut. Colonel, 30th Dec., 1828, Unatt.; Colonel, 23rd Nov., 1841; Major General, 20th June, 1854; aptd. Colonel of the 75th Regt., 22nd March, 1858; Lieut. General, 11th April, 1860; General, 8th March, 1867
11th Oct., 1853, 98th Regt.	Bt. Major, 23rd Oct., 1860; Major, 20th May, 1868, 98th Regt.
... ...	Retired 17th Dec., 1847 Aptd. Paymaster of the Rifle Brigade, 1st December, 1854; Hon. Captain, 1st Janury, 1860; died at Cawnpore, 8th July, 1864
... ...	Died in Dublin, 12th Oct., 1854

NAME.	ENSIGN, &c.	LIEUTENANT.
Coates William	4th April, 1794, 1st Foot Grds.	22nd May, 1797
Cockburn *Sir* Francis	16th Oct., 1800, 7th Dragoon Guards	6th April, 1803, 60th Regt.
Served in South America, in 1807; in the Peninsula, in 1809, 1810; and in Canada, from 1811 to 1814		
Collum William	15th March, 1855, 28th Regt.	30th Nov., 1855, 28th Regt.; exchd. to 94th, 17th July, 1857
Cooke James	4th April, 1805	1st January, 1806
Served in the Peninsula; present at Fuentes d'Onor, Ciudad Rodrigo, severely wounded at Salamanca.		
Cotton Corbett	9th April, 1825, 19th Regt.; aptd. to 16th Lancers, 29th June, 1826	29th March, 1827, 16th Lancers
Coward Isaac Toogood	25th Dec., 1813, Waggon Train; placed on h. p. of it, 1814; aptd. to 1st Vet. Batt., 25th Oct., 1822; aptd. to 94th, 1st Dec., 1823	... ...
Cox Robert Wingfield	15th May, 1855	23rd March, 1858
Craig William Alexander	3rd Dec., 1803, 44th Regt.	11th April, 1805, 44th Regt.
Creswell Eastcourt	February, 1808	21st July, 1808
Crooke George William	May, 1808	28th September, 1808
Crozier George	18th Oct., 1798, 44th Regt.	19th Dec., 1799, 44th Regt.
Cullen William	31st Aug., 1774, 53rd Regt.	2nd March, 1776, 53rd Regt.
Culley Fred. Wynyard H.	30th October, 1828	... ...
Cullinan Henry Valentine	9th Nov., 1858, 86th Regt.	22nd April, 1862, 86th Regt.; exchd. to 94th, 28th April, 1863
Cuninghame Henry Mont.	5th April, 1833	21st April, 1837; exchd. to 29th Regt., 29th Dec., 1837
Cuninghame *Sir* Thomas Montgomery, *Bt.*	15th August, 1826	28th Sept., 1830

94TH REGT.

CAPTAIN.	HIGHER RANKS, AND REMARKS.
... ... 3rd March, 1804, 16th Batt. of Reserve ; aptd. to 94th, June, 1804 ; exchd. to 3rd Drags., 14th Nov., 1804 ; exchd. to 60th Regt., 23rd April, 1807	Died at Seringapatam, July, 1799 Major, 27th June, 1811, Canadian Fencibles ; Lieut. Colonel, 27th October, 1814, New Brunswick Fencibles ; placed on h. p, of the Regt., 24th Feb., 1816 ; aptd. Dep. Major General in Canada, 25th Dec., 1817 ; exchd. to 2nd West India, 30th July, 1829 ; Local rank of Colonel at Honduras, 3rd Sept., 1829 ; Colonel, 10th Jan., 1837 ; Major General, 9th Nov., 1846 ; aptd. Colonel of the 95th Regt., 26th Dec., 1853 ; Lieut. General, 20th June, 1854 ; General, 12th Nov., 1860 ; died at 19, East Cliffe, Dover, 24th August, 1868
22nd Feb., 1861	Retired 30th December, 1864
27th Feb., 1812 ; retired on f. p. of the Regt., 17th Feb., 1814	Died 31st August, 1826
4th May, 1832, 2nd West India ; aptd. to 94th, 9th Aug., 1833	Major, 5th June, 1844 ; exchd. to 49th Regt., 6th Dec., 1844 ; Lieut. Colonel, 20th April 1849, Unatt.; Colonel, 28th Nov., 1854 ; Major General, 6th July, 1863
... ...	Removed the Service, 6th July, 1824
19th Dec., 1862	Retired 3rd January, 1865
7th July, 1814, 44th Regt.; placed on h. p. of it, 25th March, 1816 ; exchd. to 84th Regt.; 25th July, 1816 ; placed on h. p. of it, 25th Feb., 1818 ; exchd. to 68th Regt., 23rd April, 1818 ; aptd. to 50th Regt., 5th Nov., 1818 ; exchd. to h. p. of York Chasseurs, 2nd Dec., 1819 ; aptd. to 1st Vet. Batt., 25th Oct., 1822 ; aptd. to 94th, 1st Dec., 1823 ; aptd. to 2nd Vet. Batt., 20th Jan., 1825	Died at Coleraine, 21st November, 1825
... ...	Retired 1809 ; died at Malmsbury, 1828
... ...	Retired 18th January, 1810
16th Jan., 1812, 44th Regt.; placed on h. p. of it, 25th March, 1816 ; aptd. to 94th 1st Dec., 1823	Retired 21st February, 1828
13th Sept., 1781, 53rd Regt.; placed on h. p. of it, 1783 ; exchd. to 94th Regt., 17th Oct., 1799	Bt. Major, 1st March, 1794 ; Bt. Lieut. Colonel, 1st Jan., 1800 ; died in India, 11th April, 1807
... ...	Cashiered March, 1832
... ...	Retired 3rd August, 1866
... ...	Retired 31st December, 1841
... ...	Retired 5th April, 1833 ; aptd. Lieut. Colonel of the Ayrshire Militia, 2nd April, 1850 ; resigned, 14th Sept., 1858

94TH REGT.

NAME.	ENSIGN, &c.	LIEUTENANT.
Daniell Charles Augustus (*Medal for China.*) Was present at the attack and capture of Amoy, Chusan, and Chinkiang-foo. Served with the Gold Coast Artillery with the Expedition against the Crobboes during October and November, 1858.	18th Jan., 1839, 55th Regt.	10th April, 1840, 55th Regt.; exchd. to 94th, 10th October, 1845; exchd. to 75th Regt., 7th April, 1854
D'Arcy Geo. Abbas Kooli Present on the Staff during the operations of a field-force in the Southern Mahratta country in 1844 and 1845, under Major-General De la Motte.	21st April, 1837	26th September, 1839
Daunt William Thomas	21st Jan., 1826, Unatt.; aptd. to 94th, 23rd Oct., 1828; appointment cancelled, 5th February, 1829	... ...
Davenport Chas. Edgecumbe	11th Sept., 1840; aptd. to 1st Foot, 15th Dec., 1840	14th July, 1843, 1st Foot
Davenport Wm. Davenport	17th Oct., 1826, 29th Regt.	8th October, 1829, h. p. of 47th Regt.; exchd. to 94th, 29th October, 1829
Day William Dean Hoare Guinness	3rd March, 1848	24th January, 1851
De Bathe *Sir* Wm. P., *Bt.* (*Medal for* 22, 24.) Defence of Sicily. 1808; present at Washington, Baltimore, and New Orleans.	17th Dec., 1807, 4th Garr. Batt.; aptd. to 27th Regt., 3rd March, 1808	21st Sept. 1809, 27th Regt.
⚔ Deere Joseph Eyles (*Medal for Ava.*) Served the campaign of 1815 as storming of Cambray, and capture paign of 1842 in Affghanistan, including valley, and those of the 22nd and	3rd August, 1820, 72nd Regt.; placed on h. p. of it; aptd. to 41st Regt., 31st Oct., 1822 Volunteer with the 91st Regt., in of Paris; Burmese war of 1824-25, ing the action of 28th March (wound-29th May, near Candahar.	4th Nov., 1825, 41st Regt. cluding the battle of Waterloo, under Sir Archibald Campbell; cam-ed), and 28th April in the Pisheen
Dennis John Leslie (*Medal for China.*) (*Medal for India.*) Served with the 49th Regt. in and Amoy; after which he was em-and desperate band of insurgent them, killing a European officer and pany of the 94th and 100 Sepoys of nam Coonettos, in Malabar. On the swords, and war knives, rushed out the destruction of the entire Mopla received a contusion on the chest and paign of 1857-58, including the siege	25th April, 1828, 49th Regt. China (Medal), and was present at ployed as a military magistrate at fanatics having defeated a native force several Sepoys, Major Dennis, with the Madras Native Infantry, encoun-approach of our troops these mad-upon the detachment, and a sangui-band, 64 in number, three of whom a few slight wounds. Served with and capture of Delhi, and command-	22nd Sept., 1830, 49th Regt. Chusan (both operations), Canton Chusan. In Aug. 1849, a determined which had been marched against a force consisting of Grenadier Com-tered them at a Pagoda near Teerma-men, armed with matchlocks, spears, nary conflict ensued, terminating in were killed by Major Dennis, who the 52nd Lt. Inf. in the Indian cam-ed the reserve column at the assault.
Denny Peter	25th Nov., 1802	... ...
Desborough Lawrence	10th April, 1825, 3rd Foot	3rd August 1827, 3rd Foot
Dillon Robert (*Medal for Sebastopol.*) (*Sardinian Medal.*) (*Turkish Medal.*)	8th June, 1838	29th Nov., 1839; aptd. to 97th Regt., 31st Dec., 1841
Donald James (*Medal for Seringapatam.*) Wounded at Argaum.	April, 1795, 67th Regt.	3rd June, 1795
Donald Thomas	73rd Regt.	20th January, 1805
Donald William	21st December, 1809	12th March, 1812, 12th Foot

CAPTAIN.	HIGHER RANKS, AND REMARKS.
2nd May, 1850, Unatt.; aptd. to Gold Coast Artillery, 29th May, 1857	Major, 23rd July, 1861, Unatt.
9th November, 1846	Major, 6th July, 1852, 3rd West India; Lieut. Colonel, 7th July, 1854, 3rd West India; Colonel, 7th July, 1857; retired 7th May, 1858; aptd. Governor of the Gambia
... ...	Retired March, 1832
6th July, 1852. 1st Foot	Retired 30th March, 1855; aptd. Adjutant of the 1st West York Militia, 21st April, 1855; resigned, 13th October, 1858
22nd July, 1836	Major, 9th Nov., 1846; exchd. to 26th Regt., 30th April 1847; retired 1st Oct., 1847; aptd. Lieut. Colonel Commandant of the 2nd Cheshire Militia, 5th April, 1853
... ...	Died at Cannanore, Madras, 5th October, 1851
5th March, 1812, 3rd West India; exchd. to 94th, 30th July, 1812; exchd. to 85th Regt., 25th January, 1813	Bt. Major, 27th October, 1814; Major, 24th June, 1819; 85th Regt.; Lieut. Colonel, 9th April, 1825, 85th Regt.; exchd. to 53rd Regt., 28th Feb., 1828; exchd. to h. p. Unatt., 2nd April, 1829; exchd. to 8th Foot, 25th Sept., 1835; retired 2nd October, 1835
8th August, 1841, 41st Regt.; exchd. to 94th, 6th May, 1843	Died at Chatham, 16th December, 1846
17th March, 1841, 49th Regt.	Major, 29th Nov., 1844, 49th Regt.; exchd. to 94th, 6th Dec., 1844; Bt. Lieut. Colonel, 2nd Aug., 1850; Colonel, 28th Nov., 1854; Lieut Colonel, 29th Dec., 1854; exchd. to 52nd Regt., 24th Oct., 1856; Major General, 28th Oct., 1864
... ...	Retired 25th June, 1803
14th October, 1842, 3rd Foot; exchd. to 94th, 30th June, 1843	Retired 13th April, 1849; aptd. Lieut. North Devon Yeomanry, 27th May, 1854; Captain, 8th May, 1866
30th Nov. 1849, 97th Regt.; exchd. to 30th Regt., 25th July, 1851	Major, 15th Feb., 1856, 30th Regt.; retired on h. p. of it, 20th June, 1865 : Bt. Lieut. Colonel, 3rd Sept., 1867
27th January, 1804	Aptd. Paymaster of the Regt., 1808; retired on h. p., 25th March, 1810; died at White-hill, near Glasgow, 6th April, 1831, of wounds received at Argaum, in 1803
... ... 31st December, 1825, Unatt.	Died at Aberdeen, 27th September, 1838

C

94TH REGT.

NAME.	ENSIGN, &c.	LIEUTENANT.
Dore William Henry	8th December, 1857	29th September, 1839
Dorehill, George	20th Nov., 1838, Ceylon Rifles; exchd. to 97th Regt., 7th Dec., 1838	25th Sept., 1840, 97th Regt.; exchd. to 94th, 12th March, 1841
Douglas James	... ...	... ...
Douglas Queensberry	... ...	10th July, 1793
Drew Francis Barry	23rd May, 1845, 28th Regt.; exchd. to 40th Regt., 12th February, 1847	17th August, 1848, 40th Regt.
Drummond Duncan	9th April, 1780, 95th Regt.	17th Aug., 1782, 95th Regt.; disbanded 1783, placed on h. p. of it; aptd. to 35th Regt., 25th September, 1787
Durant Celestine George	24th Nov., 1852	29th Dec., 1855, 79th Regt.
Durie William S.	20th Jan,, 1832, 6th Foot; aptd. to 94th, 9th March, 1832	8th May, 1835; exchd. to 83rd Regt., 11th Aug., 1837
Du Vernet Francis Tudor Campbell	10th Nov., 1865	
Edwards Charles Frederick	16th Nov., 1841, 41st Regt.; aptd. to 24th, 19th Nov., 1841	... .
Elliot Arthur Charles	23rd Nov., 1852	29th Dec., 1854, 18th Foot; re-aptd. to 94th, 26th Jan., 1855
Elliot Francis Hamilton	26th January, 1855	14th September, 1855
Elliot John Mitchell	10th Oct., 1863, 100th Regt.; aptd. to 94th, 24th Nov , 1863	3rd August, 1866
Erskine Henry	20th Jan,, 1790, 1st Foot	20th July, 1792, 1st Foot
Erskine John	27th September, 1808	18th Jan., 1810; exchd. to 7th Fusiliers, 10th Nov., 1813
Estwick Frederick	22nd February, 1839	8th Oct., 1841; exchd. to 47th Regt.. 26th April, 1844
Ewing Patrick	26th Sept., 1787, 29th Regt.	28th July, 1790, 29th Regt.
Fair Thomas	4th November, 1813	... ...
Farrer Henry	12th Nov., 1858, 3rd West India; aptd. to 94th same day	19th December, 1862
Farrington Donald Macleod	17th Dec., 1847; aptd. to 98th Regt., 7th Jan., 1848	28th Aug., 1849, 98th Regt.
Ferrier Ilay	30th Oct., 1764, Scotch Brig. in Dutch service	... ...
Served in the Dutch Service till old Brigade formed on the British auxiliary brigade under the Dutch officers, retired to England, and in upon the British Establishment.	1782 when as Lieut. Colonel he Establishment and bearing British Ensign and having Dutch uniform. 1793 was appointed to re-raise the	resisted the attempt to change the colours and uniform into a foreign Resigned his commission with other Scotch Brigade for service wholly

94TH REGT. 19

CAPTAIN.	HIGHER RANKS, AND REMARKS.
17th Dec., 1846; exchd. to h. p. Unatt., 5th June, 1857 15th March, 1853; exchd. to h. p. Unatt., 20th May, 1853	Bt. Major, 1st Nov., 1858; retired October, 1867; died at 27, Hova Villas, Cliftonville, Brighton, 24th December, 1868
10th July, 1793; aptd. to 7th Vet. Batt., 5th May, 1804; reduced 1814, pled. on retired f. p. of it; aptd. to 3rd Vet. Batt., 7th July, 1815; reduced 24th May, 1816, placed on retired f. p. of it	Bt. Major, 29th April, 1802; died at Balgonie Cottage, Fifeshire, 8th July, 1820
25th June, 1803	Died 1804
21st Nov., 1851, 40th Regt.; exchd. to 64th Regt., 16th Jan., 1852; exchd. to 11th Foot, 16th Dec., 1853; aptd. to 94th, 26th Jan., 1855; aptd. Adjutant of a Depôt Batt., 23rd August, 1859	Bt. Major, 27th July, 1863; Major, 23rd August, 1865, Unatt.; aptd. to 8th Foot, 2nd September, 1868
24th Jan., 1791, Indpt. Company, placed on h. p. of it, 1791; aptd. to Scot. Brig., 8th July, 1793	Major, 6th April, 1797; retired 19th January, 1800; died in Edinburgh, 1st October, 1813
... ...	Retired 1st July, 1859
... ...	Retired 25th May, 1838
... ...	Died at Negapatam, Madras, 25th May, 1844
15th June, 1860; exchd. to 17th Foot, 29th March, 1861	Retired 2nd September, 1862
28th December, 1860	Died at Jullundur, East Indies, 29th March, 1863
28th October, 1794; exchd. to 91st Regt., 16th June, 1801	Bt. Major, 18th Nov., 1798; Bt. Lieut. Colonel, 25th Sept., 1803; Major, 1st Sept., 1804, 1st Foot; exchd. to York Light Infantry Volunteers, 17th July, 1806; retired, 25th July, 1806
... ...	Retired 13th January, 1814; died 23rd November, 1824
... ...	Retired 10th February, 1854
24th Jan., 1791, Indpt. Company; disbanded 1791; aptd. to Scotch Brig., 9th July, 1793	Bt. Major, 1st Jan., 1798; retired 10th September, 1799
... ...	Drowned, 6th November, 1814
26th Oct., 1855, 19th Foot; placed on h. p. of the Regt., Nov., 1856; aptd. to 4th Foot, 23rd Oct., 1857	Died at Sattara, East Indies, 15th Jan., 1866
28th Oct., 1772, Scotch Brig. in Dutch service	Major, 30th July, 1776, Scotch Brig. in Dutch service; Lieut. Colonel, 5th July, 1793; Colonel, 3rd May, 1796; Major General, 29th April, 1802; aptd. Lieut. Governor of Dunbarton Castle, 2nd July, 1796; died at Dunbarton, 6th April, 1824

NAME.	ENSIGN, &C.	LIEUTENANT.
Ferrier James Served at Seringapatam & throughout the Mahratta and Polygar wars.	March, 1794, Indpt. Company	29th March, 1794, 98th Regt.
Fielding William Hoyle	12th April, 1827	... ...
Finucane George Thurles *(Medal for Bhurtpore.)* *(Medal for Ava.)* *(Cross of St. Fernando.)* Served with the Austrian army in Italy in 1814, and was present at the surrender of Genoa. Aptd. Major in the 2nd Regt. of the British Legion of Spain, 4th Aug., 1835; afterwards Lieut. Colonel.	22nd Sept, 1808, 14th Foot	15th March, 1810, 14th Foot
Fisher William	29th January, 1836	9th June, 1838
Fisher William James	11th Feb., 1862, 49th Regt.	18th Oct., 1864, 49th Regt.; ex. to 91th, 24th June, 1867
Forster John Hill	16th Aug., 1804, 82nd Regt.	7th Nov., 1805 ; exchd. to 14th L. D., 15th Jan., 1807
Fraser Andrew	10th February, 1796	4th August, 1799
Fraser Lionel	24th Nov., 1843 ; aptd. to 95th Regt., 25th June, 1844	7th May, 1847, 95th Regt.
Frederick C.	11th April, 1805, 74th Regt.	27th March, 1806
French Caulfield	6th Nov., 1857, 92nd Regt.; aptd. to 94th, same day	12th July, 1859
French Cudbert, K.H. Served in the Peninsula in 1813 and 1814, was present at Nivelle, Nive, Orthes, and Toulouse ; besides other minor affairs.	3rd Sept., 1812, 23rd Fusiliers	1st April, 1814, 23rd Fusiliers ; placed on h. p. of the Regt., 25th Dec., 1814 ; aptd. to 94th, 15th June, 1815 ; plcd. on h. p. of the Regt., 25th Dec , 1818 ; exchd. to 18th Regt.; 25th March, 1819
Frend Albert	31st Jan., 1834, 55th Regt.	25th Aug., 1837, 55th Regt.; aptd. to 94th, 22nd Oct., 1839
Froom George	3rd Oct., 1866, 4th West India	22nd Aug., 1868, 4th West Ind.; ex. to 94th, 14th Oct., 1868
Gardiner Thomas George	15th May, 1847, 40th Regt.	12th Aug., 1849, 40th Regt.
Gascoyne Charles	7th Dec., 1820, 54th Regt.	30th Jan., 1823, 54th Regt.; aptd. to 94th, 1st December, 1823
Gaskell Gerald Milnes	19th April, 1864, 1st Dragoons ; aptd. to 62nd Regt., 4th Nov., 1864	7th August, 1867, 62nd Regt.; exchd. to 94th, 1st August, 1868
Gaskell William Plumer	21st Sept., 1852	29th December, 1854

CAPTAIN.	HIGHER RANKS, AND REMARKS.
6th May, 1795	Major, 23rd Oct., 1800 ; Lieut. Colonel, 13th Aug., 1802; died at Jaulnah, 27th September, 1804
... ...	Retired 15th January, 1829
17th June, 1828, Unatt.; aptd. a Sub-Inspector of Militia in the Ionian Islands, 3rd July, 1828 ; placed on h. p. of it, 25th June, 1830 ; aptd. to 2nd West India, 27th April, 1832 ; aptd. to 94th, 16th Jan., 1835 ; exchd to h. p., Unatt., 2nd Oct., 1835 ; ex. to 38th Regt., 23rd April, 1839, exchd. to h. p. of 36th Regt., 3rd May, 1839	Bt. Major, 28rd Nov., 1841 ; Major, 30th July, 1847, Unatt.; Bt. Lieut. Colonel, 11th Nov., 1851 ; retired on full pay, 14th July, 1857 ; rank of Colonel, same day
10th May, 1844	Retired 6th October, 1848 ; aptd. Barrack Master at Malta, Aug 1859; Curragh of Kildare, Aug. 1864 ; Gibraltar, April, 1865
... ...	Retired 18th June, 1812
10th April, 1807 ; aptd. to 6th Vet. Batt., 15th Feb., 1810 ; disbanded 1814, placed on retired f. p. of it, aptd. to 7th Vet. Batt., 1st Nov., 1819 ; disbanded 1821, placed on retired full pay of it	Aptd. Fort Major, at Inverness, 2nd Sept., 1813 ; died there, 20th December, 1846
6th June, 1854, 95th Regt.	Killed in the trenches before Sebastopol, on the night of the 31st August, 1855
6th Oct., 1808, 60th Regt.; ex. to 35th Regt., 25th May, 1809	Died of wounds received at Ter Veer, Walcheren, July 1809
30th December, 1864	
10th June, 1824, 18th Regt.; exchd. to 28th Regt., 2nd March, 1826	Major, 22nd June, 1832, 28th Regt.; Lieut. Colonel, 19th Dec., 1834, 28th Regt.; died at Kurrachee, 7th Jan., 1843
... ...	Retired 25th February, 1848
5th Nov., 1852, 40th Regt.; ex. to 94th, 1st May, 1855	Major, 21st Sept., 1860, Unatt.; aptd. to 3rd Foot, 22nd Oct., 1861 ; Lieut. Colonel, 9th Dec., 1864, 3rd Foot
31st December, 1825	Major, 23rd Aug., 1831 ; Lieut. Colonel, 22nd Oct., 1839 ; exchd. to 6th Foot, 30th March, 1841 ; placed on h. p. of the Regt., 15th April, 1842; exchd. to 72nd Regt., 25th Feb., 1845 ; exchd. to h. p. of 17th Regt., 11th Sept., 1849 ; Colonel, 11th Nov., 1851 ; Major General, 3rd April, 1858 ; aptd. Colonel of the 89th Regt., 4th July, 1864 ; Lt. General, 25th Nov., 1864
1st April, 1859 ; exchd. to 24th Regt., 5th Aug., 1859	Major, 13th Feb., 1867, 24th Regt. ; placed on h. p. of it, 23rd December, 1868

NAME.	ENSIGN, &c.	LIEUTENANT.
Gillespie William	... ...	... ...
Godfrey William Fermor	8th July, 1856	13th April, 1859; ex. to 36th Regt., 23rd March, 1860; ex. to 2nd Foot, 8th July, 1862
Goodridge Frederic Talbot	4th April, 1865	
Goodhew John	19th December, 1800	... .
Gordon Cosmo	6th Dec., 1792, 71st Regt.	28th October, 1794
Served at the siege of Pondicherry, battle of Argaum, siege of Asscerghur, Gawilghur, and various other hill forts; Walcheren expedition, 1809.		
Gore *Hon.* Saunders	5th Nov., 1802, 11th Foot	25th Sept., 1803, 57th Regt.
Wounded at Vittoria.		
Gouldhawke James	1st December, 1806	8th April, 1807
Grant James	11th October, 1800	
Grant Lewis	... ...	29th July, 1795
Grant Robert	31st October, 1794	10th February, 1796
Gray William	2nd Nov., 1809, Royal African Corps	20th Dec., 1810, Royal African Corps
Grey *Hon.* Henry Booth	12th March, 1823, 65th Regt.;	13th April, 1826, 65th Regt.; exchd. to h. p. of 71st Regt., 21st Aug., 1828; exchd. to 8th Hussars, 21st Nov., 1828
Griffiths John Charles	15th Oct., 1807, 4th Garr. Batt.	20th July, 1809, 4th Garr. Batt.; ex. to 94th, 30th Nov., 1809
Present at the defence of Cadiz; passage of the Coa, near Sabugal, severely wounded at the battle of blockade of Pampeluna, repulse of	pursuit of Massena, action at Resiege and capture of Ciudad Rodrigo; Salamanca: capture of Madrid; the sortie from Bayonne, and battle	dinha, Condeixa, Fuentes d'Onor, siege and escalade of Badajoz, battle of Vittoria, the Pyrenees, of Orthes, and Toulouse.
Groves Stephen Percy	12th July, 1833; aptd. to 1st D. G., 11th July, 1834	23rd Dec., 1836, 1st Dragoon Guards
Guinness Arthur Blair	12th Jan., 1815, 37th Regt.	16th Dec., 1825, 41st Regt.
Gwatkin Robert Lovell	21st December, 1860	30th December, 1864
Gwynne Fred. Zimennes	15th November, 1839	22nd July, 1842; exchd. to 55th Regt., 10th Oct., 1845
Hamilton James	1st April, 1795, 84th Regt.	4th May, 1796, 84th Regt.
Haldenby Morris Robert	23rd March, 1815; exchd. to 11th Foot, 15th Jan., 1818	3rd Jan., 1822, 11th Foot
☾ Halkett Hugh, C.B., G.C.H.	18th April, 1794	15th July, 1795
(*Gold Medal for* 12, 16.) Expedition to Germany 1805-6; in April 1808 embarked with Sir cheren expedition, present at the the siege of Badajoz, siege of Burgos; in April 1813 embarked for siege and capture of Glückstadt 1814,	employed at the siege of Stralsund, John Moore's army for Gottenburg, siege of Flushing; embarked for Forts at Salamanca, action of the north of Germany, and was and was employed at the blockade of	present at the siege of Copenhagen; and from thence to Portugal; Wal-Portugal January 1811, present at heights of Moresco, and retreat from present at the battle of Göhrde; Harburg.

94TH REGT.

CAPTAIN.	HIGHER RANKS, AND REMARKS.
7th July, 1793	Bt. Major, 1st March, 1794; Bt. Lieut. Colonel, 1st Jan., 1798; retired 10th July, 1799
... ...	Retired 6th February, 1866
... ...	Retired 12th May, 1803
23rd October, 1800	Major, 12th Feb., 1807; Lieut. Colonel, 20th July, 1809, 63rd Regt.; exchd. to h. p. of 16th Garr. Batt., 8th Nov., 1810; Colonel, 12th Aug., 1819; Major General, 22nd July, 1830; Lieut. General, 23rd Nov., 1841: General, 20th June, 1854; died at Exton, Hants, 7th March, 1867
25th July, 1806, 100th Regt.; exchd. to 94th, 5th March, 1812	Murdered at Vittoria, 1813. (See Military Sketch Book, vol. i, page 173; and Eventful Life of a Soldier, p. 204, by Joseph Donaldson, late of 94th.)
5th Feb., 1801, 83rd Regt.; placed on h. p. of it, 17th March, 1803; exchd. to 1st West India, 20th June, 1805	Died 1806
... ...	Died 1799
30th July, 1818, Royal African Corps; placed on h. p. of it, 1812; aptd. to 94th, 1st Dec., 1823	Bt. Major, 7th March, 1822; Major, 25th May, 1826, Unatt.; retired December, 1826
17th Dec., 1830, Unatt.; exchd. to 94th, 8th March, 1831; retired on h. p., Unatt., 9th August, 1833	
7th July, 1814; placed on h. p. of the Regt., 25th Dec., 1818	Aptd. Fort Major, at Newfoundland, July, 1830; Bt. Major, 10th Jan., 1837; died at Calais, 8th Feb., 1845
12th June, 1840, 1st Dragoon Guards	Retired 20th November, 1840
30th Dec., 1826, 41st Regt.; aptd. to 94th, 17th Dec., 1829	Retired 6th March, 1835; died at Sandford, near Dublin, 18th March, 1835
... ...	Died at Mussourie, East Indies, 1st June, 1865
... ...	Retired 30th December, 1845
31st Oct., 1803, 15th Batt. of Reserve; aptd. to 2nd Garr. Batt., 5th Dec. 1805; aptd. to 9th Vt. Batt., 1st Oct., 1807; aptd. to 6th Vet. Batt., 19th May, 1808; aptd. to 94th, 15th Feb., 1810; ex. to 3rd West India, 30th July, 1812	Dismissed the service, January 1813
... ...	Died 1825
... ...	Major, 1st July, 1805, 2nd Light Infantry, K.G. Legion; Bt. Lieut. Colonel, 1st January, 1812; Lieut. Colonel, 22nd Sept., 1812, 7th Line Batt.; placed on h. p. of it, 25th April, 1816; retired 1826; died in Hanover, 1863

94TH REGT.

NAME.	ENSIGN, &c.	LIEUTENANT.
Hall Henry Samuel	31st July, 1857	17th June, 1859 ; ex. to 32nd Regt., 18th May, 1860
Harness Wm. Edmondes	15th September, 1854	12th Jan., 1855 ; ex. to 28th Regt., 17th July, 1857 ; aptd. to 6th Foot, 23rd Oct., 1857
Harness Wm. Edmondes Re-entered the Army.	4th Sept., 1860, Canadian Rifles	18th January, 1867, Canadian Rifles
Hart Thomas Frederick	2nd January, 1823, 63rd Regt.; aptd. to 13th Light Dragoons, 5th Feb., 1824	8th April, 1826, 13th L. D.; aptd. to 1st Life Guards, 24th May, 1828
Hartley Bartholomew Present at the surrender of Martinique, and the taking of Guadaloupe.	15th Jan., 1813, York Rangers	26th May, 1814, York Rangers; placed on h. p. of the Regt., 15th Oct., 1819 ; aptd. to 2nd Vet. Batt., 21st Aug., 1823 ; aptd. to 94th, 1st Dec. 1823
Hartley Richard Wilson	26th Oct., 1841, 8th Foot	27th Sept., 1844, 8th Foot
Hassard Francis John	26th Sept., 1860	20th May, 1864
Havelock Thomas	27th Sept., 1815, 43rd Regt.; placed on h. p. of it, 25th March, 1817 ; aptd. to 60th Regt., 10th March, 1825	1st Nov., 1827
Hawke Stanhope, *Lord*	17th July, 1823, 65th Regt.	12th May, 1825, Unatt.; exchd. to 8th Foot, 29th Dec., 1825
Hawkshaw Travers	20th July, 1815, 58th Regt.; ex. to 94th, 7th Sept., 1815 ; placed on h. p. of the Regt., 25th Dec., 1818 ; aptd. to 54th Regt., 4th March, 1836	... ...
Hay George	24th Feb. 1788, 1st Foot; exchd. to 53rd Regt., 2nd April, 1788	19th Feb., 1793, 53rd Regt.
Hearn Robert Thomas	19th August, 1844	29th May, 1847 ; exchd. to 26th Regt., 31st Dec., 1847
Hedley George Lake	12th Oct., 1852, Ceylon Rifles ; aptd. to 94th, 3rd March, 1854	29th December, 1854
Hewett Simon Goodman	4th Sept., 1800, 81st Regt.	11th Feb , 1801, 81st Regt.; ex. to 94th, 30th July, 1801
Heycock Charles Hensman	3rd Aug., 1860 ; aptd. to 75th Regt., 11th Sept., 1860	9th Dec., 1864, 75th Regt.
Hill Richard Bingham	17th Nov., 1814, 21st Fusiliers; placed on h. p. of the Regt., 25th March, 1816 ; exchd. to 94th, 25th Oct., 1827	24th July, 1828, 41st Regt.
Hook Charles Campbell	29th Nov., 1839	... ...
Humpage Charles Warren	10th April, 1866	
Humphrey James	14th May, 1804, 14th Light Dragoons	8th May, 1805, 14th L. D.; ex. to 94th, 15th Jan., 1807
Humphreys John	10th July, 1860	... ...
Hunt John Edward	31st Jan., 1805, 59th Regt.	26th Feb., 1806, 26th Regt.; exchd. to 4th Garr. Batt., 8th Aug., 1811; ex. to 7th Foot, 7th May, 1812 ; ex. to 94th, 10th Nov., 1813 ; ex. to h. p. of 47th Regt., 23rd Feb., 1815

94TH REGT.

CAPTAIN.	HIGHER RANKS, AND REMARKS.
17th April, 1866, 32nd Regt.; ex. to 6th D. G., 10th July, 1866	Retired 23rd July, 1858
6th Sept., 1831, Unatt.; exchd. to 94th, 30th March; 1832	Retired 16th August, 1842; died at Wollongong, Australia, 2nd February, 1868
17th April, 1835, Unatt.	Aptd. Paymaster of the 99th Regt., 30th Oct., 1835; aptd. Paymaster of the 48th Regt., 12th May, 1837; aptd. Paymaster of the 8th Foot, 17th Dec., 1841; died in Burton Crescent, London, 9th September, 1854
9th Feb. 1849, 8th Foot; ex. to 94th, 16th Jan., 1857	Retired 31st July, 1857
... ...	Died 28th August, 1865
... ...	Retired 18th Nov., 1831; aptd. Captain in the 5th Regt. of the British Legion of Spain, 31st August, 1835; died at Vittoria, of fever, 31st December, 1835
26th Sept., 1826, Unatt.; ex. to 94th, 24th July, 1828; aptd. to 47th Regt., 28th Sept., 1830; exchd. to h. p. Unatt., 2nd Dec., 1831	Retired 8th July, 1836
29th October, 1794	Killed at Seringapatam, 26th April, 1799
... ...	Aptd. Paymaster of the 76th Regt., 30th Sept., 1851; Hon. Major, 1st Jan., 1860; died at Paisley, 6th January, 1862
18th Jan 1859; exchd. to 24th Regt., 10th Dec., 1859; ex. to 6th Dragoons, 28th Jan., 1862	Retired 20th September, 1864
... ...	Retired March, 1805
14th Oct., 1868, 75th Regt.	
... ...	Died 1838
... ...	Retired 11th Sept., 1840; aptd. Cornet, 7th Madras Native Cavalry, 1st July, 1841; Lieut., 31st Aug., 1845; Captain, 2nd July, 1851; Major, 16th April, 1863
... ...	Aptd. Quarter-master of the 85th Regt., 24th Nov., 1863
... ...	Died in Dublin, 15th July, 1827

D

NAME.	ENSIGN, &C.	LIEUTENANT.
Hutchison John	12th April, 1809	27th December, 1810
Ingle John	13th April, 1858; aptd. to 78th Regt., 24th Dec., 1858	... ...
Ingles Walter Lawrence (*Medal for Goojerat.*) Served with the 32nd Regt., at the second siege of Mooltan in 1848-9, including the storm and capture of the city, and surrender of the fortress; also present at the subsequent surrender of the fort and garrison of Chenoite, and at the battle of Goojerat.	21st January, 1848, 67th Reg.; aptd. to 32nd Regt., 25th Feb., 1848	8th October, 1850, 32nd Regt.; exchd. to 94th, 14th October, 1852; aptd. to 74th Regt., 29th July, 1853
Innes Alexander (*Silver Medal for Toulouse.*) Served in the Peninsula, and was wounded at Toulouse.	19th July, 1810, 42nd Regt.	15th Oct., 1812, 42nd Regt.; placed on h. p. of it, 25th March, 1817; aptd. to 94th, 1st Dec., 1823; placed on h. p. Unatt., 25th Nov., 1828
Innes Gordon C.	12th May, 1808	31st August, 1809
Innes John Wounded at Seringapatam, as Polygar wars, and at the defence of Cadiz.	... . Subaltern of the Grenadier Company,	27th July, 1794 served during the Mahratta and
Innes William	3rd February, 1804	13th May, 1805
Irwin William Arthur	6th Oct., 1798, 33rd Regt.	14th November, 1799
Jackson George	31st May, 1792, 35th Regt.	30th April, 1793. 35th Regt.
Jackson James Severely wounded at Vittoria.	12th May, 1812	30th March, 1815; placed on h. p. of the Regt., 25th Dec., 1818; aptd. to 19th Regt., 13th Feb., 1827; ex. to h. p. of 8th Foot, 6th March, 1828
Jackson John Napper (*Silver Medal for* 11, 14, 15, 16, 18, 22, 25, 26) Served in the Peninsula from 1810 Vedras, Massenas retreat from Por-Lis, Guarda, Foz d'Arouce, and Retiro, and Fort la China, and in Fort la China *en route* to Ciudad Bigorre and Tarbes, and all the	1st July, 1805 to the end of the war 1814, including fugal, actions and affairs at Pombal, Sabugal; actions at El Boden and command of an escort of the third Rodrigo. Retreat to Portugal, Oct. various minor affairs during that	1st January, 1806 the siege of Cadiz, Lines at Torres Redinha, Leira, Condeixa, Fleur-de-Guinaldo, capture of Madrid, the Division in charge of the garrison of and Nov. 1812, actions at Vic period.
Jameson Henry	23rd March, 1849	21st Sept., 1852; aptd. to 74th Regt., 29th July, 1853
Johnstone Wm. Geo. Currie	8th August, 1865, 66th Regt.; aptd. to 94th, 12th Sept., 1865; aptd. to 10th Foot, 20th October, 1865	
Jones Henry	25th September, 1860	24th Nov., 1863; exchd. to 62nd Regt., 1st Aug., 1868
Jones Thomas	20th Feb., 1835, 41st Regt.	16th June, 1837, 41st Regt.; ex. to 94th, 15th June, 1838
Kelly Edward Hy. Moore	10th Sept., 1830, 29th Regt.	31st July, 1835, 29th Regt.; exchd. to 94th, 29th Dec., 1837

CAPTAIN.	HIGHER RANKS, AND REMARKS.
16th Feb., 1815 ; placed on h. p. of the Regt., 25th March, 1817 ; exchd. to 83rd Regt., 20th Aug., 1818 ; aptd. to 82nd Regt., 12th Nov., 1818	Retired 4th December, 1823
... ...	Retired, June 1861
7th Sept., 1858, 16th Foot	
... ...	Appointed a Military Knight of Windsor, October, 1867
... ... 10th July, 1799	Killed at Salamanca, 22nd July, 1812 Major, 27th Sept., 1804 ; died at Portsmouth, 27th Aug., 1810, of liver complaint, a few hours after landing from Lisbon
... ... 11th April, 1807	Died at Cadiz, 1810 Retired 18th July, 1811 ; died in Jersey Major, 14th Oct., 1794, 96th Regt.; reduced, but retained on f. p. of it, 1795 ; placed on h. p. of it, 1798 ; Bt. Lieut. Colonel, 1st Jan., 1800 ; aptd to 85th Regt., 17th May, 1800 ; exchd. to 94th, 3rd April, 1801 ; exchd to h. p. of Argyleshire Fencibles, 7th April, 1802 ; exchd. to 99th Regt., 25th August, 1809 ; retired 3rd May, 1810
... ...	Retired May, 1832 ; died at St. Mary's, Jamaica, 1835
28th Feb., 1812 ; placed on h. p. of the Regt., 25th Dec., 1818 ; exchd. to 43rd Regt., 30th March, 1820 ; placed on h. p. of it, 25th Oct., 1821 ; aptd. to 99th Regt., 25th March, 1824	Major, 11th June, 1829, 99th Regt.; Bt. Lieut. Colonel, 23rd Nov., 1841 ; Colonel, 20th June, 1854 ; Major General, 26th October, 1858 ; aptd. Colonel of the 3rd West India Regt., 13th August, 1862 ; aptd. Colonel of the 99th Regt., 8th June, 1863 ; died at St. Helier's, Jersey, 25th January, 1866
... ...	Died at Bellary, 7th October, 1862
25th April, 1845	Died in consequence of a fall from his horse, at Fort St. George Madras, 28th May, 1847
22nd July, 1842 ; exchd. to 3rd Foot, 30th June, 1843 ; ex. to h. p. Unatt., 10th Dec., 1847 ; exchd. to 89th Regt., 2nd February, 1849	Retired 2nd Feb., 1849 ; aptd. Major in the Essex Rifle Militia, 23rd Oct., 1855 ; Lieut. Colonel, 2nd Feb., 1858

94TH REGT.

NAME.	ENSIGN, &c.	LIEUTENANT.
Kelly James Graves	11th Sept., 1863, 3rd West Ind.; aptd. to 94th, 24th Nov. 1863	
Kenny Courtenay W. Aylmer Thomas (*Medal for Sebastopol.*) Severely wounded at the attack of the Quarries.	23rd June, 1854, 88th Regt.	16th Nov., 1854, 88th Regt.
Keogh Francis Gethings (*Silver Medal for* 18, 19, 22, 24, 25, 26.)	9th Feb., 1809, 14th Light Dragoons	29th March, 1810, 14th L. D.; exchd. to 57th Regt., 7th March, 1811; exchd to h. p. of the Regt., 9th July, 1818; ex. to 94th, 1st April, 1824; exchd. to h. p. of 60th Regt., 10th Nov., 1825; exchd. to 86th Regt., 27th Feb., 1829
King Anthony Wright	24th July, 1828	... ...
King Edward Hammond	10th May, 1851, Newfoundland Comp.; aptd. to 94th, 31st Oct., 1851; aptd. to Ceylon Rifles, 3rd March, 1854; aptd. to 27th Regt., 7th April, 1854	2nd Feb., 1855, 7th Fusiliers; aptd. to 83rd Regt., 28th August, 1857
Kingdom Edward From Serjeant-Major, 33rd Regt. Present at the storming of Seringapatam, served in the Peninsula, and was present at the storm of Badajoz.	14th April, 1800	19th March, 1802
Kingdom John Ayres	26th Nov., 1818; placed on h. p. of the Regt., 25th Dec., 1818; reaptd. to f. p. of it, 1st Dec., 1823	10th Feb., 1825, 31st Regt.; aptd. to 64th Regt., 1st Nov., 1827
Kirby Wm. Humphreys (*Medal for India.*) Was attached to the Head Quarders of the Army under Lord Clyde, during the campaign in Oude of 1858-59 until the termination of the war.	14th October, 1836	28th December, 1838 as assistant Quarter Master General,
Kirkman James (*Silver Medal for* 10, 14, 15, 16, 18, 19, 22, 24.) Served with the Rifle Brigade including the actions and defence of aldo and Aldea de Ponte, siege and capture of Badajoz (volunteered, battle of Salamanca. advance to and Munos and San Milan, battle of to Pampeluna. which ended in the various actions in the Pyrenees, and passage of the Nive. Served	31st Dec., 1794, 122nd Regt.; placed on h. p. of 128th Regt.; aptd. to 52nd Regt., 3rd May, 1809 during the campaigns of 1810, 11, Cadiz, siege of Tarragona, battle of capture of Ciudad Rodrigo (volun- and accompanied the forlorn hope, capture of Madrid, subsequent re- Vittoria, and three days' severe capture of their last gun; action at battle of Nivelle (gun-shot wound in also the campaign of 1815 in Belgium.	25th Aug., 1809, 95th Regt. 12, 13, and 14, in the Peninsula, Barrosa, actions near Fuente Guin- teered the storming party), siege and and was wounded in the head), treat through Spain, affairs of San skirmishing in following the enemy Echalar, passage of the Bidassoa, the right arm), action of Arcangues,
Kirwan Richard (*Silver Medal for Talavera.*) Severely wounded at Talavera.	... ...	27th Oct., 1807, 7th Fusiliers
Knight Rice Davies	25th April, 1845	25th February, 1848
Knox John Hunter	30th March, 1858; aptd. to 84th Regt., 10th Sept., 1858	8th Feb., 1861, 84th Regt.; exchd. to 14th Hussars, 26th Nov., 1861

CAPTAIN.	HIGHER RANKS, AND REMARKS.
26th October, 1855, 88th Regt.; exchd. to h. p. of Gold Coast Corps, 2nd May, 1856; aptd. to 94th, 23rd Sept., 1859	Retired 28th December, 1860
2nd Nov., 1830, Unatt.; exchd. to 29th Regt., 17th April, 1835	Retired 31st July, 1835; died at Buffalo, 9th January, 1854
... ...	Retired 24th April, 1835; aptd. Major in the 3rd Regt. of the British Legion of Spain, 26th August, 1835; died of fever at Vittoria, 17th April, 1836
... ...	Aptd. Paymaster of the 59th Regt., 10th Aug., 1855; retired 16th October, 1857
19th April, 1810	Retired 26th November, 1818
29th Nov., 1837, 64th Regt.	Retired 20th December, 1839
7th December, 1845	Major, 29th Dec., 1854; Bt. Lieut. Colonel, 26th April, 1859; Colonel, 29th Dec., 1864; placed on h. p. 18th April, 1868; aptd. Adjutant General at Bombay; Lieut. Colonel, 17th April, 1868, Unatt.
18th Nov., 1813, 4th Garr. Batt.; afterwards 2nd; placed on h. p. of it, 24th Oct., 1816; aptd. to 2nd Vet. Batt., 25th Oct., 1822; aptd. to 94th, 1st Dec., 1823; exchd. to h. p. of 6th Foot, 9th Dec., 1824	Retired 12th Dec., 1826; aptd. Barrack Master at Jamaica, 8th Nov., 1839; at Sheffield, 28th March, 1842; at Richmond Barracks, Dublin, 12th Jan., 1848; died at Kingston, Dublin, 1864
16th March, 1815, 7th Fusiliers; placed on h p. of the Regt.; 25th Feb., 1816; ex. to 6th Foot, 1st May, 1821; placed on h. p. of it, Oct. 1821; ex. to 94th, 9th Dec., 1824; ex. to h. p. Unat., 24th July, 1828	Died at Brighton, 6th January, 1853
9th January, 1858, 12th Foot; exchd. to 98th Regt., 16th March, 1858	Retired 17th Dec., 1858; aptd. Adjutant of the 2nd Warwick Militia, 18th Dec., 1858
2nd Oct., 1866, 14th Hussars	

94TH REGT.

NAME.	ENSIGN, &c.	LIEUTENANT.
Knox Charles Henry	8th April, 1826, Unatt.; exchd. to 95th Regt., 14th Dec., 1826	9th Aug., 1827, 89th Regt.; placed on h. p. of it, 1829; exchd. to 85th Regt., 7th July, 1829
Kyle Alexander (*Gold Medal for Vittoria.*) (*Silver Medal for* 11, 14, 15, 19, 22, 24, 25, 26.) Present at the defence of Cadiz, and Sabugal; slightly wounded at Laing Thomas (*Gold Medal for* 22, 25) Served throughout the Peninsula	4th July, 1805 lines of Torres Vedras, actions at Ciudad Rodrigo; severely wounded 3rd June, 1795 war; severely wounded at Ciudad	7th April, 1807 Redinha, Casal Nova, Foz d'Arouce, at Badajoz; action at Vic Bigorre. 10th Feb., 1796 Rodrigo.
Lang John Sibbald	9th Nov., 1809	... ...
Lecky Clement	30th August, 1831	24th April, 1835
Leech Robert Stockham Brydges	8th October, 1855	29th Oct., 1858, 24th Regt.
Leicester Henry	10th July, 1793, 3rd Light Dragoons	2nd June, 1794, 3rd Light Dragoons
Leslie Shirley Conyers	29th December, 1814	... ...
Lewis Richard	28th July 1825, Unatt.; exchd. to 94th, 20th July, 1826	30th October, 1828
Lewis Richard Hull Served with the Grenadier Company of the 94th in the action with and destruction of a desperate band of insurgent fanatics at Teermanam Coonnettos in Malabar.	29th December, 1846	3rd March, 1848
Lindsay George Topp Present at the capture of the Isle of France.	21st Dec., 1808, Royal African Corps	21st, Sept., 1809, Royal African Corps; aptd. to 22nd Regt., 23rd Nov., 1809
Lindsey Henry John	5th Dec., 1811, 11th Foot	11th Jan., 1816, 11th Foot; placed on h. p. of the Regt., 25th March, 1816; aptd. to 94th, 9th April, 1825; ex. to h. p. Unatt., 31st Jan., 1828
Lloyd Thomas (*Gold Medal for* 16, 18.) See remarks in Napier, Book xxiii,	1st Aug., 1797, 54th Regt. Chap. 1.	6th May, 1799, 54th Regt.
Locke Wadham	3rd August, 1866	
Longworth David Fitzgerald (*Medal for Ghuznee & Cabool.*) (*Medal for the Sutlej.*) Present at Moodkee, Ferozeshah, Buddewal, Aliwal, and Sobraon, where he had his horse shot under him.	3rd May, 1831, 33rd Regt.	27th Nov., 1835, 3rd Foot; exchd. to 94th, 5th Feb., 1836
Lorimer Robert	12th June, 1812; placed on h. p. of the Regt., 25th May, 1816	... ...
Lumsden Alexander	25th Feb., 1804	14th May, 1805; exchd. to 80th Regt., 22nd Sept., 1807
Lyster Septimus Aptd. Ensign in the 3rd Regt., of and was present in the operations in the attack upon the fortified M'Alister Angus	28th December, 1838 the British Legion of Spain (Westbefore San Sebastian, and was heights of Arambura, near Hernani, 20th April, 1815; pl. on h. p. of the Regt., 25th Dec., 1818	18th Aug., 1841 minster Grenadiers) 15th June 1836, severely wounded through the body 16th March, 1837. ... ...

94TH REGT. 31

CAPTAIN.	HIGHER RANKS, AND REMARKS.
4th March, 1836, 85th Regt.; exchd. to 94th, 15th July, 1836; exchd. to h. p. Unatt, 10th Feb., 1838; ex. to 1st West India, 30th Nov., 1855	Retired 30th November, 1855
11th October, 1810, placed on h. p. of the Regt., 25th Dec., 1818; aptd. to 26th Regt., 21st July, 1854	Bt. Major, 22nd July, 1830 ; Bt. Lieut. Colonel, 9th Nov., 1846; retired 4th August, 1854 ; died at Aberdeenshire,
24th Dec., 1804	Major, 6th Jan., 1814 ; retired 16th Feb., 1815
... ...	Killed at Badajoz, 7th April, 1812
... ...	Retired 27th April, 1838
16th Jan., 1863, 24th Regt ; exchd. to 22nd Regt., 10th Nov., 1865	Retired March 1866
30th June, 1795, 3rd L. D.; exchd. to 94th, 14th Nov., 1804 ; exchd. to 28th Regt., 4th July, 1805	Retired 7th November, 1805
... ...	Retired 6th November, 1817
8th Oct., 1841 ; exchd. to 45th Regt., 20th Oct., 1843	Died at Gibraltar, 30th September, 1844
26th March, 1858, 20th Regt.; retired on h. p. of the Regt., 2nd May, 1865	Aptd. Staff Officer of Pensioners, 10th March, 1865
27th Dec., 1820, 22nd Regt.; placed on h. p. of it, 25th Oct., 1821 ; aptd. to 94th, 1st Dec., 1823	Bt. Major, 10th Jan., 1837 ; Major, 22nd October, 1839 ; died at Trichinopoly, Madras, 21st April, 1844
... ...	Died at Cork, 20th October, 1861
8th October, 1803, 6th Batt. of Reserve; aptd. to 43rd Regt., 10th Aug. 1804	Major, 4th October, 1810 ; Bt. Lieut. Colonel, 17th Aug., 1812 ; killed at the passage of the Nivelle, 10th Nov., 1813
27th Sept., 1839; exchd. to 40th Regt., 27th Aug., 1841; ex. to 31st Regt., 16th Aug., 1843; exchd. to h p. Unatt., 17th Sept., 1850 ; exchd. to 27th Regt., 7th April, 1854	Bt. Major, 19th June, 1846 ; retired 7th April, 1854
... ...	Died 24th June, 1819
... ...	Died 2nd May, 1812
6th October, 1848	Major, 18th Sept., 1857 ; Lt. Colonel, 16th Sept., 1868
.. ..	Died at Belnakill House, Argyleshire, 1839

94TH REGT.

NAME.	ENSIGN, &c.	LIEUTENANT.
M'Andrew John Lennox	14th December, 1838, 4th Foot	8th May, 1840, 4th Foot
M'Arthur Archibald Severely wounded at Vittoria.	2nd July, 1805	29th October, 1806
M'Arthur James	29th April, 1795	10th Feb., 1796
M'Arthur Peter	29th July, 1796	10th July, 1799
M'Callum Donald	30th October, 1794	10th February, 1796
M'Cleverty Robert	3rd January, 1828	23rd August, 1831
M'Cormick James (*Silver Medal for* 11, 14, 15.)	25th May, 1809	17th March, 1814; placed on h. p. of the Regt., 25th Dec., 1818
M'Crea Herbert Taylor (*Medal for the Kaffir War of* 1851, 2, 3.)	2nd August, 1844	17th Dec., 1846
M'Nab John (*Silver Medal for Toulouse.*)	4th July, 1811	16th Feb., 1815; placed on h. p. of the Regt., 25th Dec., 1818
M'Nab Robert Present at Vittoria, Pyrenees, Nivelle, Nive, Orthes, Vic Bigorre, and Toulouse.	15th Oct., 1812; placed on h. p. of the Regt., 25th Dec., 1818; exchd. to 3rd Foot, 10th Jan., 1821	9th April, 1825, 3rd Foot
M'Vean James	10th Feb., 1796	4th August, 1799
Mac Carthy Edwd. Dennis Justin	2nd Sept., 1845	18th Aug., 1848, 96th Regt.
Mac Carthy Justin Edward Daniel	16th Dec., 1840, 57th Regt.	29th March, 1844, 57th Regt.; excd. to 94th, 4th Dec., 1844
M'Farlan John Warden	8th Jan., 1847, Ceylon Rifles	28th April, 1848, Ceylon Rifles; aptd. to 94th, 6th June, 1851; aptd. to 74th Regt., 29th July, 1853
Mac Intosh Robert	15th July, 1813; placed on h. p. of the Regt., 25th Dec., 1818	... ...
Mac Neill Malcolm	20th May, 1777, 1st Foot	1778, 1st Foot
Macbeath William Wounded at Seringapatam.	... ...	9th July, 1793
Macdonald Robert Douglas	2nd March, 1820, 42nd Regt.; placed on h. p. of it; aptd. to 47th Regt., 13th Dec., 1821; exchd. back to 42nd Regt., 11th July, 1822	10th Sept., 1825, 42nd Regt.
Maclaine *Sir* Archibald, K.C.B. (*Silver Medal for Barrosa.*)	16th April, 1794	29th April, 1795

Mysore campaign of 1799 against Seringapatam, where he received for upwards of a year. Capture of including the battle of Ardingy, and and 4, against Scindia, Holkar, and of Gawilghur, siege of Asseerghur of severe wounds received in the and 12, including the defence of redoubt when taken possession of period Sir Archibald, with a very the enemy under Marshal Soult, who Lieut. General Sir Thomas Graham, at Barrosa and his horse killed;

Tippoo Sultan, including the battle three wounds, from the effects of the Danish settlement of Tranque- affair of Serungapore, where he was the Bera Rajah, including the storm- (wounded), and battle of Argaum. different actions from 1799 to 1804. Cadiz, and defence of Matagorda (an from the enemy), from 22nd Feb. to small force under his command, conducted the siege, and did not his men being nearly all either killed capture of Seville.

of Mallavelly, siege and storming of which he was confined in hospital bar. and the Polygar war in 1801, wounded. Mahratta war of 1802, 3, ing of Julnaghur, siege and storming Ordered home in 1804 in consequence Peninsular campaigns of 1810, 11. outwork of Cadiz, and a ruined 22nd April 1810, during which long most gallantly kept at bay 8,000 of evacuate until ordered to do so by or wounded. Dangerously wounded

94TH REGT.

CAPTAIN.	HIGHER RANKS, AND REMARKS.
17th May, 1850, 4th Foot; ex. to h. p. Unat., 9th July, 1852; exchd. to 94th, 5th June, 1857	Retired 14th Aug., 1857; died at Bayswater, 26th Oct., 1859
6th Jan., 1814; placed on h. p. of the Regt., 1814	Retired February, 1826
... ...	Retired 22nd September, 1800
... ...	Died at Jaulnah, May 1805
... ...	Died at Arnee, 5th June, 1799
9th Nov., 1838; aptd. to 79th Regt., 15th Dec., 1840	Died in London, 6th March, 1845
... ...	Died in Edinburgh, 21st March, 1858
... ...	Aptd. Paymaster of the 43rd Regt, 6th June, 1851; retired as Lieut. h. p. of 94th, 27th May, 1856; died 8th April, 1858
... ...	Died at Killin, near Callander, Perthshire, 26th June, 1854
27th May, 1836, Unatt.; exchd. back to 3rd Foot, 28th May, 1836; exchd. to h. p. Unatt., 5th April, 1838	Killed by a railway train, near Callander, 28th Nov., 1843
17th April 1804, 78th Regt.	Died at Bombay, 18th June, 1803
8th July, 1856, 96th Regt.	Retired 8th July, 1862
29th Dec., 1854; exchd. to 40th Regt., 1st May, 1855	Retired 15th February, 1861
24th June, 1856, Unatt.; aptd. to 9th Foot, 23rd Oct., 1857; exchd. to Military Train, 18th Dec., 1857; exchd. to 4th Hussars, 11th Oct., 1864	Retired 21st November, 1865
... ...	Died near Dunkeld, Perthshire, 14th March, 1845
12th April, 1780, 95th Regt.; aptd. to S. B., 4th Feb., 1795; aptd. to 6th Vet. Batt., 25th Dec., 1802; reduced 1814; placed on retired f. p. of it	Bt. Major, 1st 1794; Bt. Lieut. Colonel, 1st Jan., 1798; died at Campbell Town, N.B., 28th Sept., 1824
... ...	Died at Madras, 24th July, 1799
15th Aug., 1826, 42nd Regt.; exchd. to 94th, 15th June, 1838	Retired 27th September, 1839; aptd. Barrack Master, at Malta, Sept., 1854; died at No. 3, Esplanade, Dover, 9th Feb., 1860
22nd December, 1804	Major, 4th Oct., 1810, 87th Regt.; Lieut. Colonel, 25th January, 1813, 7th West India; placed on h. p. of the Regt., 25th April, 1816; aptd. to 14th Foot, 9th Aug., 1821; exchd. to 17th Foot, 4th Nov., 1822; exchd. to h. p. Unatt., 30th June, 1829; Colonel, 22nd July, 1830; Major General, 23rd Nov., 1841; aptd. Colonel of the 52nd Regt., 8th Feb., 1847; Lieut. General, 11th Nov., 1851; General, 5th June, 1855; died at No. 68, Cumberland-street, Hyde Park, 9th March, 1861.

E

NAME.	ENSIGN, &c.	LIEUTENANT.
Macneil, Archibald	10th Feb., 1796, Scotch Brigade	26th July, 1797, Scot. Brigade; exchd. to 75th Regt., 22nd Feb., 1800
Served in the East Indies, and in of Cotoite in Malabar, including the service in Guzerat, and was present and reduction of Brodera, and action the army under Sir John Murray.	1800 and 1801 was actively employed storm and capture of the fort of in the action of Kurrie, storm of the of the 6th Feb., 1803, on the banks	during the campaign in the district Pyche; in 1802 and 1803 was on outworks and camp at Kurrie; siege of the Mahe; afterwards served with
Mackie William, K.H.	21st March, 1805, 88th Regt.	24th June, 1806, 88th Regt.
Expedition to Buenos Ayres 1807, in 1809, and was present in nearly all led the forlorn hope at the storming consequently first for promotion.	where he received two severe the actions in which the 3rd division of the main breach of Ciudad Rodrigo,	wounds; joined the Peninsula army (under General Picton) was engaged; being at the time senior Lieut., and
Mackinlay John	22nd July, 1859	25th September, 1860
Maclean Alexander	15th March, 1839, 2nd West India; aptd. to 94th, 24th October, 1839	28th January, 1842
Magee Henry Wemyss	15th Dec., 1826, 30th Regt.	26th Nov., 1830, 30th Regt.; aptd. to 45th Regt., 10th May, 1831
Mahon Gilbert	9th November, 1838	24th July, 1841
Malim George William	23rd Dec., 1813; exchd. to 58th Regt., 7th Sept., 1815; plcd. on h. p. of it, 25th February, 1816; exchd. to 54th Regt., 7th February, 1822	26th Dec., 1822, 13th Foot
Malthus Sydenham	24th Jan., 1852, 1st West Ind.; aptd. to 94th, same day	11th August, 1854
Mason James	2nd August, 1844, 75th Regt.	30th Dec., 1847, 75th Regt.
Mason Richardson	14th April, 1813, 11th Foot; exchd. to 94th, 15th Jan., 1818; placed on h. p. of the Regt., 25th Dec., 1818	... ...
Maunsell George	11th July, 1834	8th Dec., 1837
Meade Richard Raphael (*Medal for India.*)	6th October, 1848	6th October, 1851
Present as a Volunteer with the Regt. at the relief of Lucknow Cawnpore, and action at Khudagunj;	Artillery in the action at Arga on 5th under Lord Clyde; also at the affair and commanded the Regt. during	July, 1857. Served with the 8th of 2nd and action of the 6th Dec. at the campaign in Oude in 1858-59.
Meek Jacob	21st March, 1810, York Chasseurs; aptd. to 14th Foot, 24th May, 1810	22nd Oct., 1812, 14th Foot; placed on h. p. of the Regt., Feb., 1818; exchd. back to f. p. of it, 23rd April, 1818
Served in the expedition under Lord William Bentinck in the Genoese territory in 1814, and with that under Sir Hudson Lowe in the south of France in 1815.		
Meik Alexander Crie	10th May, 1833, 41st Regt.	14th Sept., 1835, 41st Regt.; aptd. to 94th, 22nd October, 1839
Mellis Henry Whalley	6th Oct., 1858, Ceylon Rifles	19th Dec., 1862, Ceylon Rifles; ex. to 94th, 4th Aug., 1865; exchd. to 4th West India, 14th Oct., 1868

94TH REGT.

CAPTAIN.	HIGHER RANKS, AND REMARKS.
13th Aug., 1805, 66th Regt.; aptd. to 9th Vet. Batt., 16th June, 1808; made 3rd, 1815; reduced 24th May, 1816; placed on retired f. p. of it; aptd. to 4th Vet. Batt., 1st Novem., 1819; appointment cancelled, June, 1820	Bt. Major, 28th November, 1854; died at 8, Maitland-street, Edinburgh, 6th November, 1855
14th May, 1812; 88th Regt.; placed on h. p. of it, 25th March, 1816; exchd. back to f. p. of it, 26th March, 1818; exchd. to h. p. of 6th D. G., 26th October, 1826; aptd. to 94th, 28th Sept., 1836	Bt. Major, 22nd July, 1830; Major, 16th January, 1835, Unatt.; aptd. to 88th Regt., 10th Nov., 1837; retired 16th March, 1838; aptd. Lieut. Governor of the Gambia, August, 1838; died there, 17th September, 1839
23rd July, 1852; exchd. to h. p. Unatt., 20th July, 1855; aptd. Adjutant of the Preston Depôt Batt., 22nd December, 1854; aptd. Staff Officer of Pensioners, 23rd May, 1859	Bt. Major, 28th July, 1864
9th June, 1843, 45th Regt.; exchd. to 94th, 20th Oct., 1843	Died at Moulmein, Madras, 6th Dec., 1845
1st July, 1854	Retired 31st August, 1855; died at Rathmines, Dublin, 15th November, 1859
... ...	Died on passage to India, 11th September, 1834
30th March, 1863	
6th July, 1855, Unatt.; exchd. to 94th, 20th July, 1855	Retired 18th January, 1859
... ...	Died 28th November, 1865
31st Dec., 1841; exchd. to 1st West India, 16th May, 1851	Bt. Major, 20th June, 1854; retired 13th Feb., 1855; aptd. Adjutant of the Kilkenny Militia, 13th Feb., 1855; the East York Militia, 12th April, 1859; resigned 21st Feb., 1863
31st Aug., 1855; exchd. to 8th Foot, 16th Jan., 1857	Major, 15th June, 1866, 8th Foot
23rd June, 1825, Unatt.; aptd. to 94th, 18th August, 1825; retired on h. p. Unatt., 26th April, 1834; exchd. to 78th Regt., 22nd Dec., 1854	Retired 22nd December, 1854; died at Mobberley Hall, Cheshire, 15th December, 1857
29th May, 1847; exchd. to 60th Regt., 9th Nov., 1849; ex. to h. p. Unatt., 17th June, 1851	Retired 1854

94TH REGT.

NAME.	ENSIGN, &c.	LIEUTENANT.
Menzies James Stewart (*Medal for India.*) Served during the Indian Mutiny in 1858, and was present at the storm and capture of Copaul.	10th Feb., 1838	24th October, 1839
Mercer Edward Smyth (*4th Class of the Medjidie.*) (*Turkish Medal.*) Served in the Turkish Contingent cessively the 3rd (Albanians), 6th,	6th March, 1835, 31st Regt. at Varna, and in the entrenched and 8th Regiments.	11th June, 1836, 31st Regt.; aptd. to 94th, 22nd October, 1839 camp at Kertch, commanding suc-
Mercer Edward Smyth	19th March, 1861	2nd June, 1865
Millar Campbell Edmonstone	30th July, 1800	25th June, 1803
Mills Charles Jas. Conway	26th Dec., 1834, 77th Regt.	28th Aug., 1838, Unatt.; excd. to 59th Regt., 28th Dec., 1838 ; aptd. to 52nd Regt., 23rd Feb., 1839
Mills Samuel	4th Feb., 1826	3rd January, 1828
Milner Henry Robert	7th Feb., 1822, h. p. of 6th Foot ; exchd. to 34th Regt., 1st Jan., 1824	3rd Dec., 1825, 34th Regt.
Mitchell Hugh	... ...	29th July, 1795
Molle George Served in Gibraltar one year; at second time, two years; wounded at in India and Egypt, returned to in Portugal; severely wounded at was present in the actions near	1793, Scotch Brigade the Cape of Good Hope two; in the assault of Seringapatam; acted England in 1803 with dispatches, Roleia, and proceeded to England ; Oporto.	12th May, 1794 India three; in Egypt and India a as Aid de Camp to Sir David Baird served in Germany, and afterwards again returned to the Peninsula, and
Montague William Edward	14th Aug., 1860, 2nd Foot ; aptd. to 94th, 15th Jan.,1861	3rd January, 1865
Monro Hector William Bowen	9th Dec., 1813, 59th Regt.	3rd May, 1814, 7th Fusiliers; placed on h. p. of the Regt., 1816 ; exchd. to 94th, 28th Nov., 1816 ; placed on h. p. of the Regt., Feb., 1817 ; ex. to 32nd Regt., 19th June, 1817 ; exchd. to h. p. of 65th Regt., 29th May, 1823
Moore George Henry	22nd Sept., 1813, 11th Foot ; placed on h. p. of it, 25th Aug., 1821; aptd. to 94th, 7th April, 1825	28th March, 1826, 3rd Foot ; exchd. to h. p. of 66th Regt., 15th March, 1827 ; exchd. to 45th Regt., 4th Jan., 1833
Morgan Adolphus Fredk.	8th April, 1825 ; exchd. to h. p. of 88th Regt., 20th July, 1826 ; aptd. to 97th Regt., 6th March, 1828	11th June, 1830, 97th Regt.
Morris Edward	22nd July, 1836	9th Nov., 1838 ; exchd. to 54th Regt., 15th Jan., 1841
Munden Charles Blenheim	17th March, 1808	26th May, 1808, 84th Regt.
Munro David (*Silver Medal for* 11, 14, 15, 16, 18, 19, 22, 24, 25, 26.) Slightly wounded at Badajoz.	1807, 59th Regt.	1st June, 1807
Munro George Gunn	1st February, 1801	... ...
Munro James	... .	... ...
Murray John	17th Jan., 1851, 77th Regt.; aptd. to 94th, 24th January, 1851	21st July, 1854

94TH REGT. 37

CAPTAIN.	HIGHER RANKS, AND REMARKS.
15th March, 1853; aptd. to 74th Regt., 29th July, 1853	Bt. Major, 9th March, 1865; Major, 17th April, 1866, Unatt.
23rd March, 1849	Bt. Major, 13th Dec., 1860; Major, 18th April, 1868; exchd. to 85th Regt., 3rd June, 1868
... ...	Died at Umballa, 25th April, 1867.
... ...	Died near Jaulnah, October, 1804.
26th October, 1841, 52nd Regt.	Major, 22nd Aug., 1851, 52nd Regt.; Lient. Colonel, 11th July, 1856, 52nd Regt.; exchd. to 94th, 24th Oct., 1856; Colonel, 23rd March, 1861; retired on h. p. of the Regt., 18th Feb., 1862.
28th Dec., 1838, Unatt.; exchd. to 1st L. G., 30th Dec., 1842	Retired 30th Dec., 1842
12th Dec., 1826, Unatt.; exchd. to 94th, 1st May, 1828	Major, 5th July, 1833; Lieut. Colonel, 31st Dec., 1841, Colonel, 20th June, 1854; retired on f. p. of the Regt., 29th Dec., 1854; Hon. rank of Major General, same day; died at the Albion Hotel, Plymouth, 14th Jan., 1855
... ...	Retired 17th March, 1804
1st July, 1795	Major, 3rd Sept., 1803, 8th Batt. of reserve; exchd. to 9th Foot, 2nd June, 1804; Lieut. Colonel, 2nd Sept., 1808, 9th Foot; exchd. to 46th Regt., 3rd June, 1813; Colonel, 4th June, 1814; died at Belgaum, Madras, 9th Sept., 1823
... ...	Died at Ewell Castle, Surrey, 20th March, 1842
.. ..	Died at Secunderabad, 22nd May, 1835
... ...	Retired 10th July, 1835
... ...	Retired 1st April, 1842
... ...	Died 1st April, 1818
10th Feb., 1814; placed on h. p. of the Regt., 25th Dec., 1818; re-aptd. to f. p. of it, 1st Dec., 1823	Major, 9th Dec., 1828; retired 23rd Aug., 1831; died at 99, George-street, Edinburgh, 10th Nov. 1863, aged 79
28th April, 1808, 21st Fusiliers 8th July, 1793	Retired 9th January, 1812 Bt. Major, 1st March, 1794; Bt. Lieut. Colonel, 1st Jan., 1798; Major, 26th August, 1804
19th November, 1858	

94TH REGT.

NAME.	ENSIGN, &C.	LIEUTENANT.
Murray Francis (*Silver Medal for* 11, 14, 15, 16, 18, 19, 22, 24, 25, 26.) Served in the Peninsula from Jan., January to September, 1810; lines Sabugal, and El Boden, capture of	29th June, 1809	7th July, 1814; placed on h. p. of the Regt., 25th Dec., 1818
Murray Virginius	1810 to the end of the war 1814, of Torres Vedras, pursuit of Massena, action at Vic Bigorre. 22nd May, 1835, 2nd West India	including the defence of Cadiz from sena, actions at Redinha, Condeixa, 4th November, 1836, 2nd West India; aptd. to 94th, 22nd October, 1839
Nairne James Mellish (*Silver Medal for Vittoria.*) Severely wounded at Vittoria.	16th April, 1812	12th Feb., 1814, 93rd Regt.; exchd. to h. p. of 92nd Regt., 1st June, 1815
Nairne Stanford Norman M'Leod	19th Dec., 1862	29th August, 1865
Nelson Thomas L. R. (*Medal for Candahar.*) (*Bronze Star for Maharajpore.*) Had his horse shot under him at Maharajpore.	25th Nov., 1831	29th Jan., 1836, 63rd Regt.; aptd. to 40th Regt., 5th Feb., 1836
Nicholls Henry	25th July, 1811, 63rd Regt.	15th Sept., 1814, 63rd Regt.; placed on h. p. of it, 1814; ex. to 31st Regt., 8th June, 1815; pl. on h. p. of it, 25th Sept., 1817; aptd. to 1st Vet. Batt., 25th Oct., 1823; aptd. to 94th, 1st Dec., 1823
Nightingale Geoffrey	20th July, 1815, 1st Foot Grds.; placed on h. p. of the Regt., 25th Dec., 1818	Aptd. to 94th, 28th Nov., 1834
O'Brien Charles Donatus Corbett	26th March, 1823, 48th Regt.	24th Aug., 1825, 48th Regt.; aptd. to 63rd Regt., 17th Sept., 1833
Ogilvy David (*Silver Medal for* 11, 15, 16, 18, 19, 22, 25, 26.) Present at the defence of Cadiz, dinha, Condeixa, and Sabugal; cap-	18th May, 1809 lines of Torres Vedras, advance in ture of Madrid, and action at Vic	17th Feb., 1814; placed on h. p. of the Regt., 25th Dec., 1818 pursuit of Massena, action at Re- Bigorre.
Orr John	14th July, 1808, 63rd Regt.	13th Oct., 1808, 8th Garr. Batt.; aptd. to 85th Regt., 27th April, 1809; aptd. to 89th Regt., 25th Jan., 1813; ex. to h. p. of the Regt., 25th Dec., 1817; aptd. to 94th, 1st Dec., 1823; aptmnt. cancelled, Feb. 1824; aptd. to 47th Regt., 19th April, 1844
Orr John (*Silver Medal for* 16, 19.) Present at the siege of Burgos, and storming of St. Michael; retreat to Portugal; slightly wounded at Burgos, and severely at Waterloo.	3rd Oct., 1811, 42nd Regt.	29th April, 1813, 42nd Regt.; placed on h. p. of it, March, 1817; ex. to 94th, 3rd Aug., 1817; placed on h. p. of the Regt., 25th Dec., 1818; aptd. to 8th Vet. Batt., 6th July, 1820; disbanded 1821; plcd. on retired f. p. of it
Osborne Morgan	27th April, 1838	... ...
Osborne Samuel Allpress G.	10th Feb., 1825	31st Dec., 1825
Paley, Charles Thomas	4th May, 1855, 46th Regt.; aptd. to 94th, 11th May, 1855	18th Sept., 1857

94TH REGT.

CAPTAIN.	HIGHER RANKS, AND REMARKS.
... ...	Aptd. Barrack Master, at Edinburgh, October, 1829 ; died at Edinburgh Castle, 16th September, 1854
8th Aug., 1845, 3rd West Ind.; exchd. to h. p. of 86th Regt., 2nd July, 1847 ; ex. to 30th Regt., 1st June, 1849	Retired 1st June, 1849 ; died in Australia
... ...	Retired June, 1826
10th July, 1846, 40th Regt.	Major 15th Feb., 1856, 40th Regt; Bt. Lieut. Colonel, 28th Jan., 1862; died at Rutland House, Southsea, 22nd May, 1867.
9th Feb., 1838, Unatt.; exchd. back to 94th, 10th Feb., 1838 ; retired on f. p. of the Regt., 23rd March, 1849	Bt. Major 28th Nov., 1854
... ...	Retired 8th May, 1835 ; died at Wimbledon, 15th Jan., 1864
27th Sept., 1842	Retired 25th April, 1845; aptd. to the Surveyor's Department in Ceylon
... ...	Died in Edinburgh, 21st June, 1859
... ...	Retired 19th April, 1845; aptd. Barrack Master at Parsonstown, Feb., 1846; aptd. to Dublin, Jan., 1848; died there, 10th July, 1864
... ...	Aptd. Captain in the Edinburgh Militia, 20th June, 1831
... ...	Retired 22nd Feb., 1839
... ...	Died at Gibraltar, 26th Sept, 1828
... ...	Died at Murree, East Indies, 11th July, 1859

94TH REGT.

NAME.	ENSIGN, &c.	LIEUTENANT.
Paterson James (*Medal for China.*) Commanded the Grenadiers of the tions before Canton from the 24th to sung, Shanghae, Chin Kiang Foo, May to August 1855 (including the	17th May, 1821 Cameronians on the China expedition the 31st of May 1841, defence of and Nanking. Commanded the attack of the 18th June), and also 28th April, 1804, 32nd Regt.	4th Dec., 1823 tion, and was present at the operaNingpo, at Segoan, Chapoo, WooBuffs at the siege of Sebastopol from from Dec., until the close of the war. 7th May, 1805, 32nd Regt.
Paty *Sir* George William, K.C.B., K.H. (*Silver Medal for* 15, 16, 18, 19, 22, 24.) Served on the expedition to Copenof that war in 1814, including retreat mander of St. Bento d'Avis and	hagen in 1807. Afterwards in the from Madrid to Burgos, besides Knight of the Tower and Sword of	Peninsula from June 1811 to the end various minor affairs. Is a Commander Portugal.
Peacocke Thos. Goodricke	15th Aug., 1848, 19th Regt.; aptd. to 84th Regt., 6th July, 1849	9th January, 1855, 84th Regt.; aptd. to 30th Regt., 1st May, 1855
Pemberton Geo. Colclough	16th Dec., 1845, 65th Regt.; aptd. to 94th, 20th March, 1846	... ...
Penny William	1st Feb., 1806, 1st Ceylon Regt.	15th June, 1808, 1st Ceylon Regt.; exchd. to 80th Regt., 25th October, 1810
Phillips Robert Newton (*Medal for the Kaffir War of* 1851, 2, 3.)	27th May, 1836, 53rd Regt.	2nd Oct., 1840, 53rd Regt.
Philips Samuel	9th April, 1825; exchd. to h. p. Unatt., 2nd July, 1826; aptd. to 54th Regt., 27th April, 1832	2nd April, 1836 17th Foot; aptd. to 39th Regt., 22nd April, 1836
Pilkington Joseph Brabazon	18th January, 1859	15th June, 1860 ; ex. to Ceylon Rifles, 4th Aug., 1865
Pipon James Kinnard	3rd August, 1826	9th Dec., 1828
Poe James Hill	14th October, 1868	
Poole Thomas Crawford	15th Dec., 1840	10th May, 1844 ; exchd. to 57th Regt., 4th Dec., 1844 ; aptd. to 76th Regt., 22nd Dec., 1846
Pratt Henry Hamilton	25th June, 1844	9th Nov., 1846
Pratt Percy Joined the 2nd Batt. of the 47th in the Peninsula, shortly after the fall of St. Sebastian.	24th Sept., 1812, 47th Regt.	8th Sept., 1814, 47th Regt.; placed on h. p. of it, 1814 ; ex. to 94th, 23rd Feb., 1815
Preston William	4th August, 1799	
Priaulx Osmond de Lancey	4th April, 1849, 75th Regt.	4th October, 1852, 75th Regt.; exchd. to 94th, 7th April, 1854
Primrose Phillip	18th August, 1848	4th Aug., 1851 ; exchd. to 32nd Regt., 14th October, 1852
Radcliffe Tristram	21st Jan., 1807, 35th Regt.	28th Jan., 1808 ; aptd. to 52nd Regt., 18th Feb., 1808

94TH REGT.

CAPTAIN.	HIGHER RANKS, AND REMARKS.
5th April, 1831, Unatt.; exchd. to 12th Foot, 3rd May, 1831; exchd. to 26th Regt., 31st Dec., 1833	Bt. Major, 23rd Dec., 1842; Major, 31st July, 1846, 26th Regt.; exchd. to 94th, 30th April, 1847; exchd. to 3rd Foot, 16th July, 1852; Bt. Lieut. Colonel, 20th June, 1854; Lieut. Colonel, 15th May, 1855, 3rd Foot; retired 31st Dec., 1857, died at 9, St. James's-terrace, Regent's Park, 31st Dec., 1860
28th April, 1808, 32nd Regt.	Major, 2nd June, 1814, Spanish and Portuguese Staff; placed on h. p. of it, 25th Dec., 1816; Bt. Lieut. Colonel, 4th Sept., 1817; aptd. to 96th Regt., 29th Jan., 1824; Lieut. Colonel, 9th June, 1825, Unatt.; exchd. to 94th, 11th June, 1826; Colonel, 10th June, 1837; exchd. to h. p. unatt., 31st Dec., 1841; Major General, 9th Nov., 1846; aptd. Colonel of the 70th Regt., 8th May, 1854; Lieut. General, 20th June, 1854; General, 14th March, 1862; died at 24, Regent-street, Waterloo-place, 8th May, 1868
17th April, 1858, 24th Regt.; exchd. to 94th, 5th August, 1859	Retired 19th Dec., 1862
... ...	Retired 25th Feb., 1848
19th June, 1827, Unatt.; aptd. to Ceylon Rifles, 2nd Aug., 1827; aptd. to 94th, 21st Feb., 1828, exchd. to h. p. Unatt., 30th March, 1832	Died at Chatham, 4th April, 1845
12th Jan., 1844, 53rd Regt.; exchd. to 43rd Regt., 5th July, 1844	Major, 17th October, 1851, 43rd Regt.; Bt. Lieut. Colonel, 28th May, 1853; Lieut. Colonel, 29th July, 1854, 43rd Regt.; exchd. to 94th, 21st Feb. 1854; placed on h. p. of it; aptd. to Provisional Batt. at Chatham, 28th Sept., 1854; Colonel, 28th Nov., 1854; retired on h. p., 6th Feb., 1863; Major General, 8th Dec., 1867
... ...	Died at Codamore, 9th Oct., 1839
... ...	Retired 8th June, 1867
6th March, 1835; exchd. to 85th Regt., 15th July, 1836; exchd. to h. p. of 68th Regt., 31st March, 1843	Bt. Major, 9th Nov., 1846; Bt. Lieut. Colonel, 20th June, 1854; Colonel, 20th June, 1857; Major, 8th April, 1859, Unatt; died at Alne Vicarage, Yorkshire, 7th June, 1868
... ...	Died at Prince Edward's Island, 1st Jan., 1854
29th Dec., 1854; retired on h. p. of the Regt., 22nd Feb., 1861	Aptd. Staff Officer of Pensioners, 19th June, 1860
26th Nov., 1818; placed on h. p. of the Regt., 25th Dec., 1818; aptd. to 81st Regt., 8th April, 1825	Major, 29th Aug., 1826, Unatt; Bt. Lieut. Colonel, 23rd Nov., 1841; exchd. to 12th Foot, 25th Oct., 1842; retired same day; died at 8, Sion-place, Sion Hill, Bath, 21st April, 1859
31st July, 1857	Retired 30th June, 1863
... ...	Retired 1st Aug., 1856
... ...	Retired 1st Oct., 1812; died in Jamaica

F

NAME.	ENSIGN, &c.	LIEUTENANT.
Randolph John Weech	25th January, 1825	17th November, 1825
Reynolds Montagu Lyttleton Varnham	2nd Sept., 1845, 63rd Regt.	10th March, 1848
Rhodes Godfrey (*Medal for the Crimea.*) (*4th Class of the Medjidie.*) Served the campaign of 1853, and Spanish General Prim, was present Pacha's staff and accompanied the Station; present in the Tete de Pont tion, retiring with loss; was also at the abovementioned services he has of the Medjidie 4th Class, with a staff of the army in the Crimea, and Sebastopol.	19th March, 1841, 60th Regt. the spring campaign of 1854 on the at the battle of Oltenitza. Subsequently Turkish Irregular Cavalry in three when the Russians unsuccessfully the retreat of the Russians from received the Spanish Order of Isabel Sword of Honor from the Sultan. was present at the battles of Balaklava	25th June, 1844, 60th Regt. Danube as Aide-de-Camp to the quently was attached to Selim successful sorties from the Quarantine attacked and bombarded that position Giergevo and Slobodsia in 1854. For the Catholic, also the Turkish Order Served the campaign of 1854 on the klava and Inkerman and siege of
Richards Percival	12th Nov., 1858	30th June, 1863
Richards Samuel	6th Sept., 1856, 74th Regt.	1st October, 1858, 5th Foot
Richardson James	11th October, 1810	... .
Ridgeway Poltimore	31st August, 1854, 58th Regt.; aptd. to 94th, 25th Jan., 1855	19th August, 1856
Served with the expeditionary force January 1860. Served in China in of Wongkadza, the entrenched town and the walled town of Nantchow, Roberts William	against the Cabul Khail Wuzeree 1862 against the Taeping rebels, of Chepio, stockade of Nazyaaz, the and occupation of Nantchow. 1st Nov., 1839, 99th Regt.; aptd. to 94th, 31st Dec., 1841	Hill Tribes in December 1859 and present at the taking of the stockades walled cities of Kading and Tsinpoo, 10th July, 1843, 28th Regt.
Robertson Andrew Served during the whole of the Peninsular war.	4th May, 1809	10th Feb., 1814; placed on h. p. of the Regt., 25th Dec., 1818
Robertson Archibald (*Silver Medal for* 11, 14, 15, 16, 22, 24, 25, 26.) Served in the Peninsula from Jan. to September, where he was employed Redinha, Cazal Nova, Foz d'Arouce, and Tarbes; severely wounded in the Robertson James Robertson John Wounded at Argaum.	13th April, 1809 1810, to the end of the war, including as an Assistant Engineer; lines of Sabugal, El Boden, Aldea de Ponte, left arm at Orthes. ... ... December 1796, 15th Foot	6th Jan., 1814; placed on h. p. of the Regt., 25th Dec., 1818; exchd. to Ceylon Rifles, 28th Aug., 1823; aptd. to 96th Regt., 29th January, 1824 the defence of Cadiz from February Torres Vedras, actions at Pombal, La Bastide, Sauveterre, Vic Bigorre 15th July, 1795 4th January, 1797, 49th Regt.; exchd. to Scotch Brigade, 15th August, 1798
Robinson George	30th June, 1863	... ...
Rolls Josiah Robert	29th Dec., 1854	17th Aug., 1855
Ross Charles (*Silver Medal for* 14, 15, 16.)	15th March, 1810	4th Nov., 1813, 60th Regt.; placed on h. p. of it, 25th Dec., 1818; exchd. to Cape Corps, 27th May, 1824
Ross Hamilton	30th July, 1794	15th July, 1795; exchd. to 81st Regt., 30th July, 1801; pld. on h. p. of it, 1803
Russell William	25th April, 1811	... ...
Rutherford James (*Silver Medal for* 11, 18, 19, 22, 24, 25, 26.) Present at the defence of Cadiz in dinha, Condeixa, and Sabugal; pas-	15th February, 1810 1810, lines of Torres Vedras, pursuit sage of the Gave d'Oleron, and	27th Oct., 1814; ex. to h. p. of 23rd Fusiliers, 15th June, 1815 of Massena, actions at Pombal, Reaction at Vic Bigorre.

CAPTAIN.	HIGHER RANKS, AND REMARKS.
9th December, 1828	Bt. Major, 23rd Nov., 1841 ; Major, 31st Dec., 1841 ; exchd. to 57th Regt., 6th May, 1843 ; exchd. to h. p. Unatt., 21st May, 1847 ; Bt. Lieut. Colonel, 11th Nov., 1851 ; exchd. to 49th Regt., 3rd Feb., 1854 ; retired same day
... ...	Retired 8th Aug., 1856 ; died at Brompton, Middlesex, 18th Aug., 1856
20th July, 1849, 60th Regt.; exchd. to 94th, 9th Novem., 1849	Major, 19th Nov., 1858, Unatt.
... ...	Died at Guernsey, 23rd March, 1868
29th Sept., 1865, 5th Foot ; ex. to 94th, 8th Oct., 1867	
... ...	Died 3rd March, 1811
17th November, 1863	
17th Aug., 1852, 28th Regt.	Bt. Major, 2nd Nov., 1855 ; Major, 17th Sept., 1858, 28th Regt.; Lieut. Colonel, 2nd June, 1865, 28th Regt.; exchd. to 5th Foot, 30th March, 1866
... ...	Died at Ladyrig, Scotland, 17th March, 1832
30th Dec., 1834, Unatt.; aptd. to 1st West India, 21st Aug., 1835	Major, 30th Dec., 1845, Unatt.; died at Cove House, Kingstown, Dublin, 10th Feb., 1850
26th August, 1804	
... ...	Died at Bombay, 18th June, 1803
... ...	Died at Kangra, East Indies, 22nd January, 1865
21st Sept., 1860 ; exchd. to 24th Regt., 13th April, 1861	Died at Fawkham, near Dartford, Kent, 23rd Feb., 1862
30th, April, 1837, Cape Corps Cavalry	Retired 21st Feb., 1840
... ...	Died at the Cape of Good Hope, 1853
... ...	Superseded, March, 1812
... ...	Aptd. Barrack Master, at Kinsale, August, 1847 ; at Newcastle, in 1857

94TH REGT.

NAME.	ENSIGN, &c.	LIEUTENANT.
Sadleir Robinson	29th June, 1809, 63rd Regt.	5th April, 1810, 63rd Regt.; exchd. to h. p. of 1st Foot Guards, 20th January, 1820; aptd. to 94th, 1st Dec., 1823
St. Clair Thomas Staunton, C.B., K.H. (*Gold Medal for Nive*) (*Silver Medal for* 2, 3, 9, 11, 22, 24.) Attended the Governor of Demercollected to attack those colonies. Walcheren in several affairs; also regiment that took possession of the ision at Busaco. Commanded four of Pombal, Redinha, Puente de 1812 was employed organizing and he commanded the 5th Cacadores, Nive, passage of the Adour, and garden on the left of the allied posi-	12th August, 1803, 1st Foot ara nearly 400 miles up the Essequibo In 1809 was employed on the expedition present at the siege and capture of town. In March 1810 landed in flank companies on the retreat to the Murcella, Sabugal, and the celebradrilling recruits for the Portuguese and was engaged, after several hot investment of Bayonne, in which he tion during the sortie.	6th August, 1804, 1st Foot river in 1807 to disperse the Indians tion to the Scheldt, and engaged at Flushing with the Royals, the first Portugal, and served in the 3rd Divlines of Torres Vedras, in the actions ted movement upon Guarda. In army in Coimbra. In 1813 and 14 skirmishes, in the battles of Nivelle, successfully kept poossession of a
St. George Richard James Mansearg	31st May, 1855	30th March, 1858; exchd. to 3rd L. D., 15th April, 1859
St. John Charles William Sandrock	11th Feb., 1848, 24th Regt.; aptd. to 94th, 25th Feb., 1848 19th Feb., 1801	6th October, 1848 ... ...
Scott Thomas (*Medal for Seringapatam.*) Joined the army in Germany, and thal, proceeded to America in 1776, under Sir Ralph Abercromby, present of Nieuport, wounded near Premont, 1799; present at the siege and taking	20th May, 1761, 24th Regt. served the campaign of 1762, carried and served under General Burgoyne; in the affairs at Famars, siege of 24th May; served the whole of the of Seringapatam.	7th June, 1765, 24th Regt. the colours at the action of Wilhelmsserved on the Continent in 1793 Valenciennes, and of Dunkirk, siege campaign in the Mysore country in
Scott Thomas (*Silver Medal for* 11, 14, 15, 16, 18, 19, 22, 24, 26.) Served in the Peninsula with the the defence of Cadiz and Fort Matactions of Pombal, Redinha, Condd'Onor, second siege of Badajoz, Rodrigo—wounded at the assault; heights, covering the parties attackthe Retiro, retreat from Madrid into blockade of Pampeluna, battles of Tarbes, and battle of Toulouse.	25th August, 1808 94th, from January 1810 to the agorda,—three times wounded; lines deixa, Ponte de Murilla, Guarda, actions at Campo Mayor and El third siege and storm of the castle of ing the forts of Salamanca, battle of Portugal with the rearguard, subsethe Pyrenees, Pampeluna, and Niv-	28th Feb., 1812; placed on h. p. of the Regt., 25th Dec., 1812 end of that war in 1814, including of Torres Vedras, pursuit of Massena, and Sabugal; battle of Fuentes Bodon, siege and storm of Ciudad Badajoz, action of San Christoval Salamanca, capture of Madrid and quent advance, battle of Vittoria, elle; actions of Vic Bigorre and
Seale Charles Twysden	10th July, 1846, 74th Regt.; aptd. to 94th, 7th July, 1848	... ...
Seale Thomas Fownes	8th May, 1835	27th April, 1838
Seton William Carden	2nd March, 1832, 61st Regt.; ex. to 94th, 18th Jan., 1833	22nd July, 1836
Sewell Sir Wm. Hy., K.C.B. (*Silver Medal for* 5, 7, 9, 14, 15, 20, 22, 24, 25, 26.) Was appointed Aide de Camp to in 1807. Joined the Duke of Moore's army in its advance and in the Peninsula war as Aide de Camp (actions on the Coa and Agueda, with Sebastian, battles of the Nivelle, louse, besides Cavalry affairs and actions. Served twenty-eight years	27th March, 1806, 96th Regt.; aptd. to 16th L. D., 17th April, 1806 General Beresford, and proceeded Wellington's army in Portugal in its retreat to Corunna. Was with to Lord Beresford, and was present the Light Division), Busaco, sieges Nive, before Bayonne (10th, 11th, skirmishes. Had six horses killed in India.	26th Feb., 1807, 16th Light Dragoons with the expedition that left England 1808. Was present with Sir John the Duke's Head Quarters through at the battles of Corunna, Talavera of Ciudad Rodrigo, Badajoz, and St. 13th December), Orthes, and Touand wounded under him in general
Sexton Samuel	17th Dec., 1847, 2nd West Ind.; aptd. to 94th, 7th Jan., 1848	... ...
Shiel Richard	9th December, 1828	18th November, 1831
Shirreff Robert D. Forbes	18th Sept., 1857; aptd. to 8th Foot, 23rd October, 1857	1st October, 1858, 8th Foot
Simpson Francis	... ...	5th July, 1793; placed on h. p. of the Regt., 1808

94TH REGT.

CAPTAIN.	HIGHER RANKS, AND REMARKS.
3rd January, 1828	Retired 17th Dec., 1829; aptd. Major of the 1st British Batt. serving in Portugal, 1832, and was killed in action at the defence of Oporto, 21st March, 1833
30th Sept., 1807, 1st Foot	Major, 2nd June, 1814, Portuguese and Spanish Staff; placed on h. p. of it, 25th Dec., 1816; Bt. Lieut. Colonel, 4th Sept., 1817; aptd. to 94th, 29th June, 1826; Lieut. Colonel, 9th Dec., 1828, Unatt.; Colonel, 10th Jan., 1837; Major General, 9th Nov., 1846; died at 55, Gloucester-place, Hyde Park, 23rd October, 1847
... ...	Retired 1st June, 1860
17th Aug., 1855; placed on h. p., 1867	Aptd. Staff Officer of Pensioners, 1st July, 1867
... ...	Appointment cancelled, 1808
14th July, 1777, 24th Regt.; aptd. to 53rd Regt., 8th Oct., 1777	Bt. Major, 13th Nov., 1793; Lieut. Colonel, 27th October, 1794, 94th Regt.; Colonel, 1st January, 1801; Major General, 25th April, 1808; Lieut. General, 4th June, 1813; General, 22nd July, 1830; died at Malleny, Scotland, 29th April, 1842
... ...	Died 19th December, 1858
... ...	Dismissed the service, 24th January, 1851
16th August, 1842	Died at Madras, 21st August, 1849
22nd May, 1840; exchd. to 41st Regt., 6th May, 1843	Major, 15th Oct., 1847, 41st Regt.; retired 26th Nov., 1852
12th March, 1812, 16th L. D.; exchd. to 60th Regt., 29th April, 1813; placed on h. p. of it, 25th Oct., 1821; exchd. to 49th Regt., 29th May, 1828	Bt. Major, 3rd March, 1814; Bt. Lieut. Colonel, 21st June, 1817; Major, 11th Aug., 1829, 31st Regt.; Colonel, 10th Jan., 1837; Lieut. Colonel, 17th Sept., 1839, 6th Foot; exchd. to 94th, 30th March, 1841; Major General, 9th Nov., 1846; aptd. Colonel of the 79th Regt., 24th March, 1854; Lieut. General, 20th June, 1854; died at Florence, 13th March, 1862
... ...	Retired 24th November, 1852
... ...	Retired 9th June, 1838
18th Oct., 1864, 8th Foot	Retired 10th November, 1865
... ...	Died 1831

NAME.	ENSIGN, &c.	LIEUTENANT.
Skelly Gordon Served the campaign in India including Mysore. At Seringapatam Colonel Wallace commanded detachments of 74th and Scotch Brigade sent to drive the enemy from a circular fort 74th seized the circular fort, but the capture the old buildings, which were afterwards known as "Skelly's post."	28th May, 1782, 1st Foot	21st Sept., 1789, 1st Foot Seringapatam and operations in the 74th and Scotch Brigade sent to were annoyed by musketry. The was sent with the Scotch Brigade to
Sladen Ramsay Cunliffe	13th April, 1849	5th Nov.. 1852 ; aptd. to 22nd Regt., 5th Aug., 1853 ; aptd. to 27th Regt., 27th May, 1854
※ Snodgrass John James Served in the Peninsula, and was present at the Pyrenees, Vera, Nivelle, Nive, Orthes, Tarbes, and Toulouse ; Burmese war of 1824 to 1826, of which he wrote a narrative, published by Murray, 1827.	9th May, 1812, 52nd Regt	7th April, 1813, 52nd Regt.; placed on h. p. of it, 25th Dec., 1818 ; exchd. back to f. p. of it, 17th May, 1821 ; aptd. to 38th Regt., 18th October, 1821
Snow William Henry	14th Feb., 1811, 16th L. D.	2nd January, 1812, 16th L. D.; exchd to h. p. of 4th L. D., 2nd March, 1815 ; ex. to 6th Dragoons, 8th Jan., 1824
Spiller William Wounded in both thighs at Vimiera; present at the battle of Corunna; in the Peninsula from July 1811 to September 1812; expedition to Amera musket wouud on the right hand (lost little finger), severe wound in the chin, two wounds on the right thigh, and severely burnt from head Ciudad Rodrigo. (From Sergeant-Major, 43rd Regt.)	25th November 1824	6th October, 1825 Walcheren expedition 1809; served ica, present at New Orleans; received the forehead, right temple, and under to foot by the explosion of a mine at
Spooner Charles Captain, Renfrew Militia, 25th April, 1808.	12th April, 1810	... ...
Squirl William Served in India, present at th Fuentes d'Onor, second siege of Badajoz, Orthes and Toulouse.	20th October, 1796	25th October, 1799 in the Peninsula, and was present at
Stainton Joseph Severely wounded at Vittoria.	24th January, 1811	8th Nov., 1813, York Chasseurs
Stephens Nassau William	8th Nov., 1827	3rd Dec,, 1830
Steuart Ramsay	5th February, 1858	5th May, 1860
Stewart Alexander (*Silver Medal for Martinique.*)	4th May, 1807, 90th Regt.	16th Dec., 1808, 96th Regt.; made 95th, 1816 ; placed on h. p. of it, 25th March, 1819; aptd. to 2nd Vet. Batt., 25th Oct., 1823 ; aptd. to 94th, 1st December, 1823
※ Stewart Robert (*Silver Medal for 2, 3, 5.*)	31st Aug., 1805, 91st Regt.	13th May, 1808, 91st Regt.
Stehelin Edward Logan	6th August, 1858, 16th Foot ; aptd. to 94th, 10th Sept., 1858	30th March, 1863 ; ex. to 49th Regt., 24th June, 1867
Stoddard John Served in the Mahratta campaign including the actions of Mahatee and	3rd Jan., 1817, 34th Regt. of 1818, also in the Burmese war, Aracan.	7th April, 1825, 34th Regt.; exchd. to 54th Regt., 19th January, 1826
Stoddard Thomas Henry	26th October, 1841	5th June, 1844 ; aptd. to 74th Regt., 29th July, 1853

CAPTAIN.	HIGHER RANKS, AND REMARKS.
16th October, 1792, 1st Foot	Major, 27th October, 1794 ; Bt. Lieut. Colonel, 1st Jan., 1800 ; retired 3rd April. 1801 ; died at Pilmore House, Durham, 30th November, 1838
... ...	Died in India, 27th May, 1854
22nd Dec., 1825, 91st Regt.	Major, 14th Nov., 1826, Unatt.; Bt. Lieut. Colonel, 25th Dec., 1826 ; exchd. to 94th, 3rd August, 1830 ; Lieut. Colonel, 28th June, 1833, Unatt.; aptd. Deputy Quarter-master General in Nova Scotia, 12th Sept., 1834 ; died at Halifax, Nova Scotia, 14th January, 1841
16th June, 1825, Unatt.; aptd. to 94th, 8th June, 1826	Died at Devonport, December, 1827
22nd October, 1839	Retired 22nd May, 1840 ; died at Belfast, 12th May, 1841
... ...	Retired December, 1812
29th September, 1808	Retired 20th Oct., 1814 ; died at Galley Lodge, near Enniscorthy, 1839
2nd Dec., 1819, half pay of York Chasseurs; exchd. to 37th Regt., 29th March, 1821; ex. to h. p. of Sicilian Regt., 4th Aug., 1825; aptd. to 95th Regt., 8th June, 1826	Died at Corfu, 28th Oct., 1832
21st April, 1837	Retired 8th June, 1838 ; aptd. Captain in the 2nd Cheshire Militia, 30th Dec., 1854 ; resigned 30th Jan., 1861
7th April, 1825	Retired 21st April, 1837
27th April, 1820, 91st Regt.; exchd. to h. p. of 55th Regt., 31st July, 1823 ; aptd. to 94th, 21st July, 1825 ; excd. to h. p. Unatt., 1st May, 1828 ; exchd. to 1st Foot, 30th April, 1841	Bt. Major, 10th Jan., 1837 ; retired 30th April, 1841 ; died at Ardsheal House, Appin, Argyleshire, 28th March, 1851
3rd Nov., 1840, Unatt.; aptd. to 94th, 15th Dec., 1840	Died at Madras, 23rd May, 1842
10th March, 1858, 18th Foot ; transferred to Madras Staff Corps, 11th July, 1865	Major, 12th Sept., 1866, Madras Staff Corps

94TH REGT.

NAME.	ENSIGN, &C.	LIEUTENANT.
Stonehouse Hy. Vansitart	25th February, 1848	13th April, 1849 ; aptd. to 74th Regt., 29th July, 1853
Stow Frederic Milkington	3rd Jan., 1865 ; exchd. to Mil. Train, 23rd March, 1866	
Strachan James Ens., Dumfries Mil., 24th Jan., 1855. *(Medal for Oude.)* Served during the Indian mutiny Tyrhool, and the Oude campaign.	30th August, 1855, 44th Regt.; aptd. to 32ud Regt., 17th April, 1857 in 1857-59, and was present at the	1st July, 1857, 32nd Regt.; exchd. to 94th, 18th May, 1860 capture of the forts of Dehaign and
Stretch John	25th November, 1799	... ...
Sykes Joseph Alfred	31st December, 1841	2nd August, 1844
Symes William Alexander	1st June, 1860	17th November, 1863
Tate John	11th January, 1800	14th November, 1800
Taylor Arthur Sanders Dangerously wounded at Ciudad Rodrigo.	7th Nov., 1805, 66th Regt.	16th April, 1807, 6th Garr. Batt.; exchd. to 81st Regt., 21st April, 1808 ; exchd. to 94th, 11th Oct., 1810
Taylour *Lord* John Henry	14th Oct., 1849, 85th Regt.	3rd Dec., 1852, 85th Regt.
Teevan George James Served with the ?Abysinnian expedition.	24th Nov., 1857, 3rd Light Dragoons	22nd June, 1858, 3rd L. D.; ex. to 94th, 15th April, 1859
Thackwell Joseph Edwin *(Medal for Hyderabad.)* *(Medal for the Crimea.)* *(Legion of Honour.)* *(Sardinian Medal.)* *(5th Class of the Medjidie.)* Served the campaign in Scinde; vestment and capture of forts Pa- of Alma and Inkerman (horse shot)	6th June, 1834, 90th Regt. campaign of 1844-5 in the Southern nulla and Pownghur ; eastern camsiege of Sebastopol, and repulse of	23rd Oct., 1839 ; aptd. to 22nd Regt., 4th Jan., 1841 Mahratta country, including the inpaign of 1854-5, including the battles the sortie on 26th October.
Thelwall Jno. Bulkeley, C.B. *(Medal for the Punjaub.)* Present at battles of Sadoolapore, Chillianwallah, (severely wounded) and Goojerat.	4th August, 1843, 24th Regt.	3rd April, 1846, 24th Regt.
Thorne Peregrine Francis, K.H. Served in America, and was present Machias, on the river Penobscot.	16th July, 1807, 25th Light Dragoons at the attack and capture of the fort	1st January, 1809, 25th Light Dragoons and town Castine, Bangor, and
Thornton John *(Silver Medal for 11, 14, 15, 16, 18, 19, 22.)* Served in the Peninsula from Feb. September 1810, lines of Torres capture of Madrid ; and dangerously the lower part of the ear.	27th August, 1807 1810 to February 1814; including Vedras, actions at Redinha, Conwounded at Nivelle through the neck	2nd August, 1810 ; exchd. to h. p. of 42nd Regt., 17th July, 1817 the defence of Cadiz from April to deixa, Sabugal, and El Boden, and by a musket ball, which carried away
Timbrell Thos. Richardson	22nd Dec., 1813, 87th Regt.; aptd. to 94th, 7th July, 1814	26th Nov., 1818 ; placed on h. p. of the Regt.. 25th Dec., 1818 ; exchd. to 58th Regt., 25th Nov., 1819 ; exchd. to h. p. of Rifle Brigade, 14th June, 1821 ; re-aptd. to 94th, 1st Dec., 1823
Tod Robert Alexander Boothby	30th Nov., 1849	1st July, 1854
Tomkins Alexander	28th June, 1824, 2nd West India	24th Dec., 1825, 2nd West Ind.; aptd. to Ceylon Rifles, 6th May, 1836 ; aptd. to 94th, 13th May, 1836

94TH REGT.   49

CAPTAIN.	HIGHER RANKS, AND REMARKS.
... ...	Retired 25th Aug., 1854
... ...	Retired 20th May, 1864
... ... 13th April, 1849	Retired 11th Jan., 1800 Retired 17th Aug., 1855; aptd. Major in the East and North York Artillery Militia, 28th Dec., 1860; died at Raywell, near Brough, East Yorkshire, 1st Sept., 1865
... ... 13th Feb., 1814, 22nd Regt.; placed on h. p. of it, Dec., 1814; exchd. to 1st Foot, 22nd Dec., 1825 31st Aug., 1855, 85th Regt. 24th November, 1863	Died in camp, near Jaulnah, Oct., 1803 Retired 9th Aug., 1827 Major, 7th Aug., 1867, 85th Regt.; exchd. to 94th, 3rd June, 1868
26th May, 1848, 22nd Regt.	Bt. Major, 12th Dec., 1854; Bt. Lieut. Colonel, 2nd Nov., 1855; Major, 29th April, 1856, Unatt; exchd. back to 22nd Regt., same day; retired on h. p. Unatt., 8th July, 1856; Colonel, 25th June, 1861
21st Dec., 1849, 24th Regt.; exchd. to 94th, 13th April, 1861; transferred to Bengal Staff Corps, 17th Nov., 1863	Bt. Major, 26th April, 1859
13th August, 1813, 60th Regt.	Major, 24th Feb., 1817, 60th Regt., placed on h. p. of it, 15th March, 1817; aptd. to 94th, 1st Dec., 1823; exchd. to h. p. Unatt, 3rd Aug., 1830; Bt. Lieut. Colonel, 10th Jan. 1837; exchd. to 44th Regt., 16th April, 1841; retired same day
... ...	Retired 24th May, 1827
14th August, 1857	Retired 14th June, 1860
8th Dec., 1837, Unatt.; exchd. to 77th Regt., 9th Dec., 1837	Bt. Major, 11th Nov., 1851; died at Florence, 24th Nov., 1852

G

NAME.	ENSIGN, &C.	LIEUTENANT.
Topp Richard	11th June, 1812	... ...
Tovey James Tennent	23rd Nov., 1849, 24th Regt.	8th Aug., 1851, 24th Regt.
Tulloch Thomas (*Medal for the Crimea.*) (*5th Class of the Medjidie.*)	15th June, 1826	23rd October, 1828
Tweedie James Lt. Renfrew Militia, 1st May, 1805. Wounded at Nivelle, 10th Nov., 1813	18th March, 1808	27th Feb., 1812; exchd. to h. p· of 7th Fusiliers, 28th Nov., 1816
Vaughan Edward	30th Jan., 1835, 9th Foot; ex. to 94th, 17th April, 1835	... ...
Vaughan Robert Walter Newman Commanded the Grenadier Company in the action with and destruction of a desperate band of insurgent fanatics at Teermanam, Coonettos in Malabar, and was severely wounded with a spear.	16th August, 1842	25th April, 1845
Watson John	18th Aug., 1808; exchd. to 4th Garr. Batt., 24th May, 1810	20th May, 1813, 4th Garr. Bat.; made 2nd, 1814; placed on h. p. of it, 25th Dec., 1816; aptd. to 48th Regt., 10th Feb., 1832; placed on h. p. of it, 25th Dec., 1833
Watson William	29th September, 1808	23rd Sept., 1813; placed on h. p. of the Regt., 25th Dec., 1818; aptd. to 20th Regt., 27th Nov., 1821
Wahab Henry John	22nd May, 1840	16th August, 1842
Waite Thomas	5th January, 1841	... ...
Wallace John	6th March, 1835	10th Feb , 1838; exchd. to 41st Regt., 15th June, 1838
Wallace Robert Edward	17th November, 1863	26th September, 1867
Walton Norcliffe Bendyshe	22nd November, 1844	17th December, 1847
Wauchope William	14th April, 1803, 93rd Regt.; aptd. to 94th, 12th May, 1803	March, 1805
Webster William Francis	6th Feb., 1823, h. p. of 76th Regt.; aptd. to 94th, 5th February, 1829	12th July, 1833; retired on h. p. of 2nd Ceylon Regt., 13th May, 1836; aptd. Staff Officer of Pensioners, 8th Nov., 1843
Wedderspoon John Ensign, Perthshire Militia, 14th March, 1808; Lieut. 24th May, 1809.	29th August, 1811	... .
Westenra *Hon.* Richard	27th April, 1815; plcd. on h. p. of the Regt., 25th Dec., 1818; exchd. to 70th Regt., 4th January, 1821	8th April, 1825, 7th Fusiliers
Wetherall John	8th Nov., 1821, h. p. of 85th Regt.; aptd. to 94th, 1st Dec., 1823	27th Aug., 1825; aptd. to 13th Light Dragoons, 1st Nov., 1827
Whaite John Edmund (*Medal for the Punjaub.*)	18th Dec., 1847; aptd. to 10th Foot, 7th July, 1848	21st Feb., 1850, 10th Foot

94TH REGT. 51

CAPTAIN.	HIGHER RANKS, AND REMARKS.
... ...	Killed in the attack of the enemy in their fortified posts, on the left of the Gave-de-Pau, 24th February, 1814
10th Sept., 1858, 24th Regt.; ex. to 94th, 10th Dec., 1859; transferred to Bengal Staff Corps, 17th Nov., 1863	
12th July, 1833 ; exchd. to 42nd Regt., 15th June, 1838	Bt. Major 9th Nov,, 1846 ; Major, 20th May, 1853, 42nd Regt.; Bt. Lieut. Colonel, 20th June, 1854 ; Lt. Colonel, 9th March, 1855, 42nd Regt.; exchd. to h. p. Unatt., 9th October, 1855 ; Colonel, 26th Oct., 1858 ; aptd. to 1st D. G., 21st Oct., 1859; retired same day
... ...	Died 22nd September, 1843
... ...	Died at Combe-grove House, 29th Sept., 1836
... ...	Died at sea, on board the *Malabar*, at Madras, 3rd August, 1851, brought on shore and interred with military honours in St. Mary's burial ground
... ...	Died in Edinburgh, 13th February, 1847
4th July, 1834, 57th Regt.	Died on passage to Europe, 31st July, 1835
21st July, 1854	Aptd. Paymaster of the Regt., 8th December, 1854
... ...	Died at Nungaveram, ten miles from Trichinopoly, Madras, 6th June, 1844
... ...	Retired 14th February, 1840
10th March, 1858, 17th Foot	Died 28th Jan., 1859, on board the *Victoria* steamer, returning to England, from the effects of injuries received in the late steamer *Austria*
8th Aug., 1805, 22nd Regt.	Major, 14th Jan., 1813, Meuron's Regt.; Lieut. Colonel, 8th Dec., 1814, h. p. of 48th Regt.; exchd. to 31st Regt., 25th May, 1815 ; exchd. to 26th Regt., 8th June, 1815 ; exchd. to h. p. of Watteville's Regt., 23rd Oct., 1817 ; died 1826
28th October, 1853, Unatt.	Died at Manchester, 13th October, 1865
... ...	Died 1812
10th June, 1826, Unatt.; exchd. to 8th Foot, 27th Jan., 1837	Retired 3rd Feb., 1837; died at Balyleck, county Monaghan, 9th June, 1838
3rd May, 1831, Unatt.; exchd. to 41st Regt., 17th May, 1831	Died at Kurrachee, East Indies, 28th September, 1842
15th June, 1858, 10th Foot	Retired 26th April, 1864

94TH REGT.

NAME.	ENSIGN, &c.	LIEUTENANT.
Wheeler John Edwd. Hatch	1st June, 1855	1st October, 1858, 8th Foot
White Henry Parsons	6th June, 1799	
White William Grove, C.B. (*Gold Medal for 18, 19.*) Expedition to the West Indies Lucia; expedition to the Mediterradangerously in the ribs, at the White William Grove	14th April, 1795, Warde's Corps; aptd. to 48th Regt., Aug., 1795 under Sir Ralph Abercromby in nean, 1798; present at the taking of Pyrenees, where he had his horse 1st October, 1818, 48th Regt.	21st October, 1795, 48th Regt. 1795; present at the capture of St. Malta; wounded in the leg, and shot under him. 5th Sept., 1822, h. p. of 48th Regt.; aptd. to 94th, 1st Dec., 1823
Whitworth John	3rd December, 1830	6th March, 1835; exchd. to 3rd Foot, 5th Feb., 1836
Wilkin Henry John Assistant Surgeon, 13th Jan., 1852, Staff; aptd. to 11th Hussars, 23rd Jan., 1852; resigned 2nd Feb., 1855. (*Medal for the Crimea.*) (*5th Class of the Medjidie.*) (*Turkish Medal.*) (*Medal for India.*) Served in the 11th Hussars through M'Kenzie's Farm, battles of Alma, Had the honour of being called out Chief for services in the field. Served 1858 (severely wounded in the opera was present at the affair of Meen including the affair near Churda and Raptee, advance into Nepaul and Williamson James	2nd Feb., 1855, 11th Hussars out the Eastern campaign of 1854-55, Balaklava, Inkerman, and Tcher in front of the Regiment on parade in the 7th Hussars in the Indian tions before Lucknow) and from gunge, siege and capture of Lucknow, pursuit, taking the fort of Meejeedia, affair at Sitkaghat (mentioned in 28th Dec., 1804, 42nd Regt.	6th Feb., 1857, 11th Hussars; exchd. to 6th Drag. Guards, 17th July, 1857; aptd. to 7th Hussars, 14th Aug., 1857 including the affairs of Bulganac and naya, siege and fall of Sebastopol. and thanked by the Commander in campaign in February and March December 1858 to March 1859, and throughout the Byswarra campaign, attack on Bankee with pursuit to the despatches.) 25th March, 1805, 79th Regt.
Wilson Charles	27th January, 1801	15th July, 1803
Wilson Clifford	16th Oct., 1857, 36th Regt.	9th Sept., 1859, 36th Regt.; ex. to 94th, 23rd March, 1860
Wimbledon Richard	1st June, 1797, 71st Regt.; aptd. to 80th Regt., Feb. 1798	6th Feb., 1798, 75th Regt.; ex. to 94th, 22nd Feb., 1800
Workman Thomas	3rd Jan., 1811, 4th West India	2nd April, 1812, 4th West Ind.; placed on h. p. of it, 25th Dec., 1818; ex. to 65th Regt., 30th Nov., 1820; placed on h. p. of it, 4th April, 1823; aptd. to 94th, 1st Dec., 1823
Wyatt Francis Dalmahoy	11th April, 1845, 17th Foot; aptd. to 94th, 8th Oct., 1847	22nd Aug., 1849; aptd. to 74th Regt., 29th July, 1853
Yorke *Hon.* Grantham Munton	10th Aug., 1826, 52nd Regt.	15th Jan., 1829; exchd. to 85th Regt., 29th January, 1829; retired on h. p. Unatt., 30th March, 1832
Mein Frederick R. (*Medal for the Crimea.*) (*5th Class of the Medjidie.*) (*Turkish Medal*) (*Medal for China.*) Served in Canada during the re May 1855, including the battles of of 1860 in China, and was present at the 2nd Batt. on the advance, and	22nd Oct., 1833, 1st Foot bellion of 1838-39. Served the cam Alma and Balaklava, and siege of the taking of Sinho and Tangku, was present at the surrender of	14th April, 1837, 1st Foot paign of 1854, and up to the 3rd Sebastopol. Served the campaign occupation of Tientsin; commanded Pekin.

94TH REGT. 53

CAPTAIN.	HIGHER RANKS, AND REMARKS.
... ...	Died at Meeanmeer, 17th Sept., 1853
14th April, 1804, 48th Regt.	Major, 25th Nov., 1809, 48th Regt.; Bt. Lieut. Colonel, 26th Aug., 1813; Lieut. Colonel, 2nd January, 1817, 48th Regt; placed on h. p. of it, 25th Dec., 1818; aptd. to 94th, 1st Dec., 1823; retired 10th June, 1826; died at Newtown College, Swanage, Dorsetshire, 3rd March, 1844
... ...	Discharged by sentence of Court-martial, held at Gibraltar, 6th July, 1824
... ...	Died at Meerut, Bengal, 9th March, 1838
19th April, 1864, 7th Hussars; exchd. to 94th, 19th April, 1864; exchd. to 48th Regt., 30th January, 1865	Bt. Major, 20th May, 1864; retired 4th Dec., 1866
8th June, 1809, 79th Regt.; ex. to 94th, 18th Jan., 1810	Killed at Ciudad Rodrigo, 19th January 1812
3rd April, 1866; exchd. to 5th Foot, 8th Oct., 1867	
... ...	Died 1807
3rd Aug., 1830; exchd. to h. p. Unatt., 8th March, 1831	
10th Sept., 1858, 24th Regt.; exchd. to 2nd West India, 8th July, 1859; exchd. to 90th Regt., 12th March, 1861	Died at Calcutta, 27th December, 1861
... ...	Retired June, 1833; took holy orders, 1844; aptd. Prebendary of Lichfield; Rural Dean; Rector of St. Philip's, Birmingham
3rd May, 1844, 1st Foot	Bt. Major, 7th Sept., 1855; Major, 30th March, 1858, 1st Foot; Bt. Lieut. Colonel, 3rd Feb., 1864; Lieut. Colonel, 1st April, 1866, Unatt.; aptd. to 94th, 17th March, 1869

NAME.	PAYMASTERS.
Donald James (*Medal for Seringapatam.*) Wounded at Argaum.	Ensign, April, 1795, 67th Regt.; Lieut., 3rd June, 1795, Scotch Brigade ; Captain, 27th Jan., 1804 ; aptd. Paymaster of the Regt., 1808 ; retired on h. p. of it, 23th March, 1810 ; died at White-hill, near Glasgow, 6th April, 1831
Fisk William Hawley Served in the Kertch campaign, 1820.	Cornet, 27th April, 1815, 1st D. G.; Lieut., 25th Oct.. 1815, 1st D. G.; reduced June, 1816, placed on h. p. of it, 25th July; ex. to 17th Lancers, 7th May, 1818 ; Capt., 8th April, 1826, 17th Lancers; ex. to h. p. Unatt , 29th June, 1826 ; aptd. Paymaster of the 17th Lancers, 19th Oct., 1826 ; ex. to his former h. p., 25th Sept., 1828 ; aptd. Paymaster of the 94th, 14th May, 1829 ; retired on h. p. Unatt., 17th Feb., 1837 ; aptd. Adjutant of the South Devon Militia, 22nd Sept., 1836 ; Bt. Major, 23rd Nov., 1841 ; Bt. Lt. Col., 11th Nov., 1851 ; aptd. to 12th Foot, 22nd Feb., 1861 ; retired same day ; aptd. Captain Comm. of the 2nd Devon (Plymouth) Volunteer Rifles ; Major 2nd Adm. Batt., Devon Volunteer Rifles, 18th September, 1863
Hewson John Mills	Ensign, 18th March, 1842, 78th Regt.; Lieut.. 29th Dec., 1843, 78th Regt.; aptd. Paymaster of the 94th, 28th Sept., 1847 ; exchd. to 35th Regt., 5th May, 1854 ; Hon. Major, 1st Jan., 1860 ; aptd. to 37th Regt., 7th August, 1867
Lukin William Smith	Deputy Assist. Com. General, 24th May, 1813 ; placed on h. p , Sept., 1822 ; aptd. Paymaster of the 94th, 8th April, 1824 ; retired on his former h. p. 14th May, 1829 ; retired June, 1832
M'Alpin William Bain	Ensign, 6th Feb., 1814, 78th Regt.; Lieut. 25th June, 1824, 78th Regt.; Capt., 3rd Aug., 1838, Unatt.; aptd Paymaster of the 94th, 22nd, Feb., 1839 ; died at sea, 14th May, 1846
Patison Matthew	Ensign, 13th July, 1815, 90th Regt.; placed on h. p. of it, Feb., 1816 ; aptd. to 99th Regt , 25th May, 1824 ; Lt., 3rd March, 1825, 99th Regt.; aptd. Paymaster of the 94th, 17th February, 1837 ; died at Cork, 29th August, 1838
Shearman William	2nd Lieut., 21st April, 1837, 87th Fusiliers ; Lieut., 5th May, 1842, 87th Fusiliers ; exchd. to 91st Regt., 25th June, 1844 ; aptd. Paymaster of the 35th Regt., 31st Jan., 1845 ; exchd. to 94th, 5th May, 1854 ; aptd. to 1st Dragoons, 4th Aug., 1854 ; placed on h. p. as Lieut. 91st Regt., 15th Feb., 1856 ; aptd. to 16th Foot, 2nd May, 1856 ; retired same day
Wahab Henry John	Ensign, 22nd May, 1840 ; Lieut., 16th Aug., 1842 ; Capt., 21st July, 1854; aptd. Paymaster of the Regt., 8th Dec., 1854
Wright James (*Silver Medal for* 11, 14, 15, 16, 18, 19, 22, 24, 25, 26.)	25th March, 1810 ; placed on h. p. of the Regt., 25th Dec., 1818; died 18th August, 1860
QUARTER MASTERS.	
Chalmers William	27th July, 1805 ; placed on h. p. of the Regt., 25th Dec., 1818 ; placed on retired f. p. of it, 1823 ; died 25th Feb., 1851
Crozier George	5th Jan., 1841 ; died at Fort St. George, Madras, 22nd Jan., 1847
Fitzgerald Thomas	23rd Jan., 1847 ; aptd. to a Depôt Batt., 1st Oct., 1856 ; placed on h. p., 14th May, 1858 ; rank of Hon. Captain, same day
Harper Thomas	21st November, 1856
Jackson William H.	18th January, 1798 ; died 1805
Mackenzie John From Colour Sergeant Rifle Brig.	1st Jan., 1834 ; retired on h. p. of the Regt., 17th Aug., 1838 ; died in London, 1st February, 1846
Waite Thomas	17th August, 1838 ; appointed Ensign, 5th Jan., 1841 ; died at Nungaveram, near Madras, 6th June, 1844

94TH REGT.

NAME.	SURGEONS.
Bennet Joseph Present at the defence of Matagorda.	Assistant Surgeon, 6th September, 1810 ; died 1811
Biddle Thomas James Served with the 49th Regt. in the Crimea from 13th Sept. to 23rd Dec., 1854. Served with the 8th Regt. at the siege and assault of Delhi, including repulse of Sorties on the 14th, 18th, and 23rd July, the capture of four guns on 12th Aug., the six days' fighting in the City, and capture of Burn Bastion.	Assistant Surgeon. 15th August, 1854, Staff ; aptd. to 94th, 1st June, 1855 ; aptd. to 8th Foot, 12th Sept., 1856 ; aptd. to Staff, 18th June, 1861 ; placed on h. p. of it, 8th Oct., 1861 (*Medal for Sebastopol.*) (*Medal for India.*)
Booth Edward	Assistant Surgeon, 11th June, 1841 ; aptd. to Military Prison at Greenlaw, 23rd Jan., 1846; Surgeon, 13th Feb., 1852, 73rd Regt.; died at Dinapore, 25th May, 1860
Brown William Accompanied the Staff all through the battle of the Alma, and was also present at other engagements.	Assistant Surgeon, 11th Sept., 1846, 3rd West India ; aptd. to Staff, 8th Dec., 1848 ; aptd. to 94th, 17th June, 1853 ; reaptd. to Staff, 15th Aug., 1854 ; Surgeon, 27th Aug., 1854, 95th Regt.; died at Scutari, 28th Nov., 1854, of fever brought on by incessant attention to the sick and wounded, and by exposure on the heights, near Sebastopol
Bulteel Edward Josias	Assistant Surgeon, 27th Oct., 1825 ; exchd. to Staff, 17th May, 1831 ; resigned January, 1833
Burkett Robt. John Baylis	Assistant Surgeon, 22nd Aug., 1811, 63rd Regt.; retired on h. p. of 7th Fusiliers, 18th January, 1816 ; aptd. to 36th Regt., 2nd June, 1825 ; aptd. to 94th, 4th May, 1826 ; died at Gibraltar, 30th July, 1828
Burrell Wm. Henry, M.D.	Assistant Surgeon, 12th April, 1821, 38th Regt.; exchd. to 72nd Regt., 18th July, 1821 ; aptd. to Staff, 29th December, 1826 ; exchd. to 94th, 17th May, 1831 ; reaptd. to Staff, 28th March, 1834 ; Surgeon, 5th May, 1837, 77th Regt.; Staff Surgeon, 1st class, 16th Dec., 1845 ; placed on h. p. 24th June, 1854 ; Deputy Inspector General, 14th Oct., 1857 ; died at Beacon-hill House, Exmouth, 31st October, 1866
Cowan Thomas, M.D.	Assistant Surgeon, 17th Sept., 1841, Staff ; aptd. to 60th Regt., 5th Oct., 1841 ; exchd. to 17th Foot, 16th March, 1849 ; Staff Surg., of the 2nd class, 5th Nov., 1852 ; reaptd. to 17th Foot, 18th Feb., 1853 ; ex. to 52nd Regt., 27th May, 1853 ; ex. to 94th, 17th July, 1857 ; died at Peshawur, 7th Nov., 1858
Cross James	Assist. Surgeon, 11th March, 1813 ; placed on h. p. of the Regt., 25th Dec., 1818 ; aptd. to 2nd Vet. Batt., 25th Dec., 1821 ; plcd. on h. p. of it, June, 1826 ; aptd. to 66th Regt., 22nd June, 1826 ; aptd. to 3rd L. D., 18th Jan., 1827 ; Surgeon, 19th Nov., 1830, 83rd Regt.; retired on h. p. of it, 5th May, 1837
Dempster James, M.D.	Assistant Surgeon, 24th Jan., 1811, 93rd Regt ; exchd. to h. p. of 81st Regt., 1st April, 1819 ; aptd. to 42nd Regt., 14th April, 1825 ; Surgeon, 27th Sept., 1827 ; retired 19th Nov., 1830 ; aptd. to 1st Tipperary Militia, 30th Sept., 1847
Dix Frederick	Assistant Surgeon, 19th Aug., 1813, 11th Foot ; retired on h. p. of Staff, 2nd April, 1818 ; aptd. to f. p. of it, 10th March, 1820 ; Surgeon, 1st Nov., 1827, Staff ; aptd. to 94th, 19th Nov., 1830; died at Cannanore, Madras, 10th July, 1840
Enright John	Assistant Surgeon, 25th June, 1802, 8th L. D.; Surgeon, 31st March, 1808, 91st Regt.; exchd. to 94th, 28th Sept., 1809 ; died in camp at Ariscoun, Spain, 23rd September, 1813 Lieut. Colonel Lloyd read the funeral service.
Fitzgerald Francis Lewis	Assistant Surg. 12th Aug., 1853, Staff ; aptd. to 86th Regt., 28th Oct., 1853 ; aptd. to 94th, 28th Nov., 1856 ; aptd. to Staff, 25th Sept., 1857 ; Surg., 29th July, 1862, Staff ; aptd. to 2nd Foot, 9th Dec., 1862 ; reaptd. to Staff, 17th Nov., 1863 ; died at Kingstown, 7th December, 1863

94TH REGT.

NAME.	SURGEONS.
Gammie Patrick (*Medal for the Sutlej.*) Present at Moodkee, Ferozeshah, Buddiwal, Aliwal, and Sobraon.	Assistant Surgeon, 17th June, 1836, 80th Regt.; Surgeon, 2nd March, 1847, 61st Regt.; exchd. to 94th, 30th Dec., 1853 ; Staff Surgeon of the 1st class, 1st May, 1855 ; Dep. Inspector General, 31st Dec., 1858 ; placed on h. p., August, 1867
Grant John Donald	Assistant Surgeon, 30th Dec., 1836, Staff ; aptd, to 94th, 13th Feb., 1846 ; dismissed the service, 11th June, 1847
Griffith Moses (*Silver Medal for 9, 11, 14, 15, 16, 18, 19, 22, 26.*) Wounded at Vic Bigorre, 19th March, 1814.	Assistant Surgeon, 24th Oct., 1811 ; aptd. to 47th Regt., 27th November, 1817; Surgeon, 8th February, 1827, 20th Regt.; retired on h. p. of it, 4th Sept., 1840
Harvey William (*Medal for Cabool.*) Served during the campaign of 1842 in Affghanistan, including the actions at the Khyber Pass, Mamoo Khail, Jugdulluck, and Tezeen, re-capture of Cabool, and taking of Istaliff.	Assistant Surgeon, 28th March, 1834 ; aptd to 9th Foot, 20th Feb., 1835 ; Surgeon, 30th July, 1844, 2nd Foot ; aptd to 70th Regt., 22nd Dec., 1848 ; died at Cawnpore, 1st Aug. 1853
Hewat Richard	Assistant Surgeon, 15th June, 1815, 21st Fusiliers ; placed on h. p. of the Regt., 25th March, 1816 ; aptd. to 94th, 27th Nov., 1817 ; placed on h. p. of the Regt, 25th Dec., 1818 ; exchd. to 46th Regt, 10th Jan., 1824 ; exchd to h. p. of 65th Regt., 22nd Nov., 1827 ; died in Berwickshire, 16th Dec., 1861
Leask James Greig, M.B.	Assistant Surgeon, 28th Aug., 1855, Staff; aptd. to 94th, 18th Sept., 1857 ; re-aptd. to Staff, 1st December, 1865
Leitch James, M.D.	Assistant Surgeon, 23rd Jan., 1846 ; aptd. to 78th Reg., 6th Feb., 1846 ; Surgeon, 1st May, 1855, Staff; exchd. to 41st Regt., 21 Nov., 1856 ; Surgeon Major, 23rd Jan., 1866 ; aptd. to 46th Regt., 7th December, 1867
Loane George	Assistant Surgeon, 4th Aug., 1808, 40th Regt.; Surgeon, 26th May, 1814 ; placed on h. p. of the Regt., 25th Dec., 1818 ; aptd. to 8th Vet. Batt., 1st Nov., 1819 ; placed on h. p. of it, 25th May, 1821 ; died in Ireland, 21st February, 1837
Lorimer William Served in the Peninsula from June 1810, to the end of the war in 1814.	Assistant Surgeon, 22nd June, 1815, 91st Regt.; placed on h. p. of it, 25th Feb., 1816 ; aptd. to 94th, 25th Dec., 1823 ; ex. to h. p. of the 6th Vet. Batt., 7th April, 1825 ; aptd. to 65th Regt., 30th April, 1829 ; Surgeon, 3rd Nov., 1837, 1st West India ; aptd. to 24th Regt., 1st June, 1838 ; exchd. to 49th Regt., 3rd April, 1846 ; retired on h. p. of it, 27th Oct., 1849; died 28th December, 1859
Lyster John	Assistant Surgeon, 10th July, 1805, South Down Militia ; aptd. to 23rd Fusiliers, 31st March, 1808 ; aptd. to 7th D. G., 14th July, 1808 ; Surgeon, 27th Jan., 1825 ; died at the Naval Hospital, Gibraltar, 14th August, 1827
M'Grath Edmund	Assistant Surgeon, 1st Aug., 1857, Staff ; aptd. to 94th, 11th Sept., 1857 ; re-aptd. to Staff, 22nd Sept., 1863 ; aptd. to 8th Hussars, 20th Sept., 1864
Martin Henry Clinton	Assistant Surgeon, 28th March, 1846, Staff ; aptd. to 87th Regt., 14th April, 1846 ; exchanged to 8th Foot, 21st April, 1846 ; aptd. to 94th. 12th Sep., 1856 ; Staff Surgeon of the 2nd Class, 11th Sept., 1857 ; placed on h. p., June, 1862 ; died 14th May, 1866
Menzies Edward	Assistant Surgeon, 29th Oct., 1841, Staff; aptd. to 20th Regt., 5th Nov,. 1841 ; aptd. to 94th. 22nd April, 1842 ; Staff Surg., 2nd Class, 26th July, 1853 ; Surgeon Major, 29th Oct., 1861 ; aptd. to 19th Hussars, 20th June, 1865 ; re-aptd. to Staff, 17th April, 1867 ; Deputy Inspector General, 4th March, 1868

NAME.	SURGEONS.
Moore Jas. Guy Piers (*Medal for the Crimea.*) (5*th Class of the Medjidie.*) (*Turkish Medal*) Present at the affair of Bulganac, battle of Alma, capture of Balaklava, sortie on the 20th October, battle of Inkerman, and siege of Sebastopol.	Assistant Surgeon, 3rd March, 1837, Staff; exchd. to 94th, 13th July, 1838 ; aptd. to 65th Regt., 22nd April, 1842 ; aptd. to 97th Regt., 23rd Sept., 1845; Surgeon, 12th June, 1846, 88th Regt ; Staff Surgeon of the 1st Class, 8th Dec. 1854 ; retired on h. p., 12th September, 1865 ; rank of Deputy Inspector General, same day
Page William John	Assistant Surgeon, 14th April, 1863, Staff; aptd. to 94th, 22nd September, 1865
Purves John Clay, M.D.	Assistant Surgeon, 9th April, 1847, Staff; aptd. to 94th, 11th June, 1847 ; exchd. to 50th Regt., 31st May, 1850 ; retired 10th Feb., 1854
Renwick Robert, M.D.	Assistant Surgeon, 9th Sept., 1813, 20th Regt.; exchd. to h. p. of 6th Vet. Batt., 15th Aug., 1816 ; exchd. to 94th, 7th April, 1825 ; superseded February, 1826
Ross Baillie	Assistant Surgeon, 20th Feb., 1806 ; Surgeon, 11th March, 1813, 50th Regt.; retired on h. p. of 1st Foot, 17th Feb., 1820 ; died 1826
Sainter James Dow	Assistant Surgeon, 1st March, 1859, Staff; aptd. to 94th, 22nd Sept., 1863 ; aptd. to Royal Artillery, 5th Aug., 1864 ; aptd. to 109th Regt., 13th Feb., 1866 ; exchd. to Staff, 23rd Oct., 1867
Scott James	Surgeon, 24th Aug., 1807 ; exchd. to 91st Regt., 28th Sept., 1809 ; aptd. to 9th Vet. Batt., 7th March, 1811 ; made 3rd, 1815 ; reduced 24th May, 1816, placed on h. p. of it ; died at Melrose, 18th January, 1837
Shelky Charles	Surgeon, 4th February, 1795 ; died in India 1799
Smith John	Assistant Surgeon, 25th Dec., 1796, 75th Regt.; Surgeon, 4th June, 1799 ; died at Madras, 24th August, 1807
Stewart Ludovick Chas. (*Medal for Punjaub.*) Present at the passage of the Chenab, and battles of Chillianwallah and Goojerat.	Assistant Surgeon, 8th June, 1841, 39th Regt ; exchd. to 50th Regt., 21st April, 1846 ; exchd. to 29th Regt., 20th July, 1847 ; Surgeon, 11th June, 1852 ; exchd. to 61st Regt., 30th Dec., 1853 ; exchd. to Staff, 3rd Jan., 1859 ; Staff Surgeon Major, 8th June, 1861 ; aptd. to 78th Regt., 20th Sept., 1864 ; Deputy Inspector General, 9th March, 1867
Still Charles Stewart	Assistant Surgeon, 26th Oct., 1832 ; exchd. to Staff, 13th July, 1838 ; resigned 17th Sept., 1839
Stoney Andrew Acres (*Medal for India.*) Served during the Mutiny of 1857-58.	Assistant Surgeon, 22nd Dec., 1848, 50th Regt ; exchd. to 94th, 31st May, 1850 ; Surgeon, 11th May, 1855 ; exchd. to 52nd Regt., 17th July, 1857 ; re-aptd. to 94th, 18th Jan., 1859 ; Surgeon Major, 22nd Dec., 1868
Thompson William, M.D. Walcheren expedition 1809; served in the Peninsula ; Kaffir war of 1819.	Assistant Surgeon, 18th Oct., 1810, 38th Regt.; aptd. to Staff, 12th April, 1821 ; Surgeon, 19th Jan., 1838, 6th Foot ; aptd. to 94th, 11th July, 1840 ; died at Madras, 27th March, 1852
Tilt Samuel	Assistant Surgeon, 1st Jan., 1801, 17th L. D.; Surgeon, 4th Feb., 1808, 87th Regt.; aptd. to 37th Regt., 9th Sept., 1813; exchd. to h. p. of 27th Regt., 5th June, 1817 ; aptd. to 94th, 25th Jan., 1824 ; reverted to his former h. p., 27th January, 1825 ; died at Bitteswell, Leicestershire, January, 1828
Turnbull William, M.D.	Assistant Surgeon, 14th Sept., 1838 ; died 14th October, 1846, on passage to England.
Turner Alexander, M.D.	Assistant Surgeon, 30th Sept., 1863, Staff; aptd. to 94th Dec., 1865 ; re-aptd. to Staff, 4th March, 1868

NAME.	SURGEONS.
Wallace John	Assistant Surgeon, 2nd June, 1857, Staff; aptd. to 94th, 25th Sept., 1857; placed on h. p. of the Regt., 22nd Sept., 1865; reaptd. to Staff, 9th March, 1867; aptd to 62nd Regt., 18th April, 1868
Watts Joseph	Assistant Surgeon, 1st June, 1855, Staff; aptd. to 94th, 1st June, 1855; aptd. to 70th Regt., 28th Nov., 1856; aptd. to 1st D. G., 23rd Nov., 1860; Surgeon, 11th April, 1868, Staff; aptd. to 59th Regt., 18th April, 1868
Westall William, M.D.	Assistant Surgeon, 21st July, 1846, Staff; aptd. to 94th, 29th Jan., 1847; died on passage from Sydney, on board the *Zenninder*, 27th January, 1853
Williams John, M.D. Present at the passage of the Douro Busaco, Fuentes d'Onor, Ciudad Rodrigo, Badajoz, Salamanca, Vittoria, San Sebastian, Orthes, and Toulouse; served in America during the latter part of the war.	Assistant Surgeon, 20th June, 1805, 52nd Regt.; Surgeon, 3rd Sept., 1812, 9th Foot; aptd. to 94th, 28th Oct., 1813; Staff Surgeon, 26th May, 1814, retired on h. p., Nov., 1838; died at Florence, 15th February, 1841
Woods George Bagnell	Assistant Surgeon, 21st Nov., 1828; retired on h. p. of the Regt., 26th Oct., 1832; died, 14th Oct., 1832

ADDENDA.

Brooke Lionel Godolphin	Ensign, 5th May, 1869, 9th Foot; aptd. to 94th same day
Davenport Wm. Davenport	Died at Bramall Hall, Cheshire, 21st Feb., 1869
Goodridge Frederic Talbot	Aptd. to 5th Foot, 3rd Feb., 1869
Lyster Septimus	Retired on h. p. of the Regt., 17th March, 1869
Mein Frederick R.	See page 52
Wahab Henry John	Honorary Major, 8th Dec., 1864

www.ingramcontent.com/pod-product-compliance
Lightning Source LLC
Chambersburg PA
CBHW031205160426
43193CB00008B/503